Frank W. Benson
The Impressionist Years

Frank W. Benson
The Impressionist Years

Essays by John Wilmerding, Sheila Dugan and William H. Gerdts

A loan exhibition for the benefit
of the Graduate School's Fellowship Fund in Art History,
Graduate School and University Center of the
City University of New York

11 May – 11 June 1988

Spanierman Gallery

50 East 78th Street   New York, New York 10021   (212) 879-7085

Published in the United States of America
in 1988 by Spanierman Gallery,
50 East 78th Street, New York, N. Y. 10021

© 1988 Spanierman Gallery

ISBN 0-945936-00-1

Contents

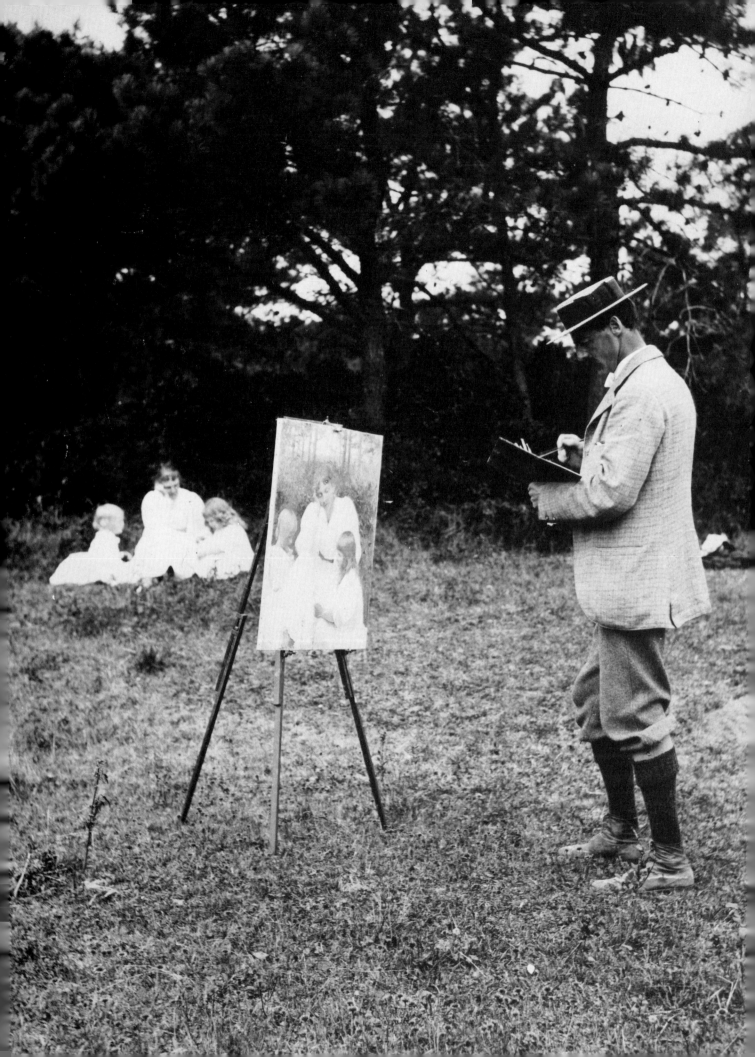

Introduction

Frank W. Benson's impressionist paintings of his children and grandchildren in the brilliant light of the North Haven, Maine, landscape have an undeniable appeal. It has always seemed to me that in these works the artist perfectly matched his love for this breezy, coastal landscape with his love for his family.

This exhibition is unique in that it is the first ever to concentrate entirely on Benson's plein-air paintings. We chose to look closely at the outdoor paintings of the artist's family and friends at or near their Maine summer home, rather than presenting an overview or retrospective of the artist's work. Seeing this group of works together, we are transported in time, drawn into a world of natural beauty and of the elegant, genteel lifestyle of the day. Our viewpoint has also allowed us to address questions of Benson's technique and approach to outdoor painting that have not been previously considered.

I wish to thank our exhibition curator, Sheila Dugan, for uncovering much new and unexplored material on Benson, and William H. Gerdts and John Wilmerding, whose essays greatly enhance our understanding of the artist. Many members of the Spanierman Gallery staff also contributed to this effort, notably David Henry, Lisa Peters, Laurene Buckley Banks, Ellery Kurtz, Christine Oaklander, Susan Kelly and Carol Lowrey. Above all, I am grateful to our lenders for providing us with this chance to experience Benson's summers in Maine.

Ira Spanierman

Opposite:
Frank W. Benson painting his wife, Ellen Peirson Benson, his daughter Eleanor, and his son George in Newcastle, New Hampshire, c. 1893. Photograph. Courtesy of the Essex Institute, Salem, Massachusetts

Acknowledgments

I would like to thank Ira Spanierman for allowing me the opportunity to organize this exhibition of Frank W. Benson's outdoor paintings. His long-standing interest in Benson and his appreciation of the beauty of the Maine works are fully realized in this show. By focusing exclusively on Benson's paintings of figures in the out-of-doors, a subject which has not previously been explored, the exhibition provides a new perspective on the artist and reveals his uniqueness.

For their assistance on this project and their constant support, I am grateful to the entire staff of the Spanierman Gallery. I have benefited greatly from Lisa N. Peters, Director of Research, who helped coordinate the exhibition and offered knowledgeable contributions to the effort. David C. Henry, Director, also gave welcome advice during every phase of this undertaking. The encouragement of Laurene Buckley Banks, Research Associate, has been invaluable to me, as were her many thoughtful recommendations for the catalogue. I am indebted to Ellery Kurtz, Registrar, who arranged the transportation and installation of the works with careful attention. Christine I. Oaklander provided generous help with the administration of the project. Special appreciation is also due to William H. Gerdts and John Wilmerding, whose insightful essays have added significantly to Benson scholarship.

Many others have given important support to this project. The catalogue was realized through the efforts of several people: Diana Murphy did an excellent job as editor; Carol Lowrey gave valuable assistance on bibliographic citations; David Sassian provided editorial consultation. David Dearinger, Amy Good, Susan Kelly, Jay Petillo and Kim Uyttewaal contributed essential help as research assistants.

For furnishing research material and photographs from the Frank W. Benson Family Papers, and for generously offering their expertise in behalf of this show, I would like to thank Eugenia A. Fountain and Prudence K. Backman, Librarians at the Essex Institute in Salem, Massachusetts. Information about the artist in North Haven was provided by Lewis Haskell of the North Haven Historical Association, Maine; Jim Pendleton, University of Southern Maine, Gorham; Mary Van Ness Crocker; and Herbert Parsons, Jr. Mary and John Brock brought maps of the area to my attention.

The greatest thanks are due, however, to those who made the works available for this exhibition. To the private lenders who parted with beloved paintings, we are sincerely grateful. The show attests to their awareness of the importance of scholarly and selective exhibitions. Numerous members of museum staffs also offered encouragement and were of great assistance in the arranging loans, notably, Dina G. Malgeri, Anthony F. Tieuli and Celia Brown of the Malden Public Library, Malden, Massachusetts; Theodore E. Stebbins, Jr., Trevor J. Fairbrother, Erica E. Hirshler and Patricia Loiko of the Museum of Fine Arts, Boston; Marilyn Solvay and Elizabeth Biddle Jennings of the William A. Farnsworth Library and Art Museum, Rockland, Maine; John K. Howat, Doreen B. Burke, Pam Hubbard and Toby Yuen of the Metropolitan Museum of Art, New York; and Janet R. Fireman of the Natural History Museum of Los Angeles County.

Sheila Dugan

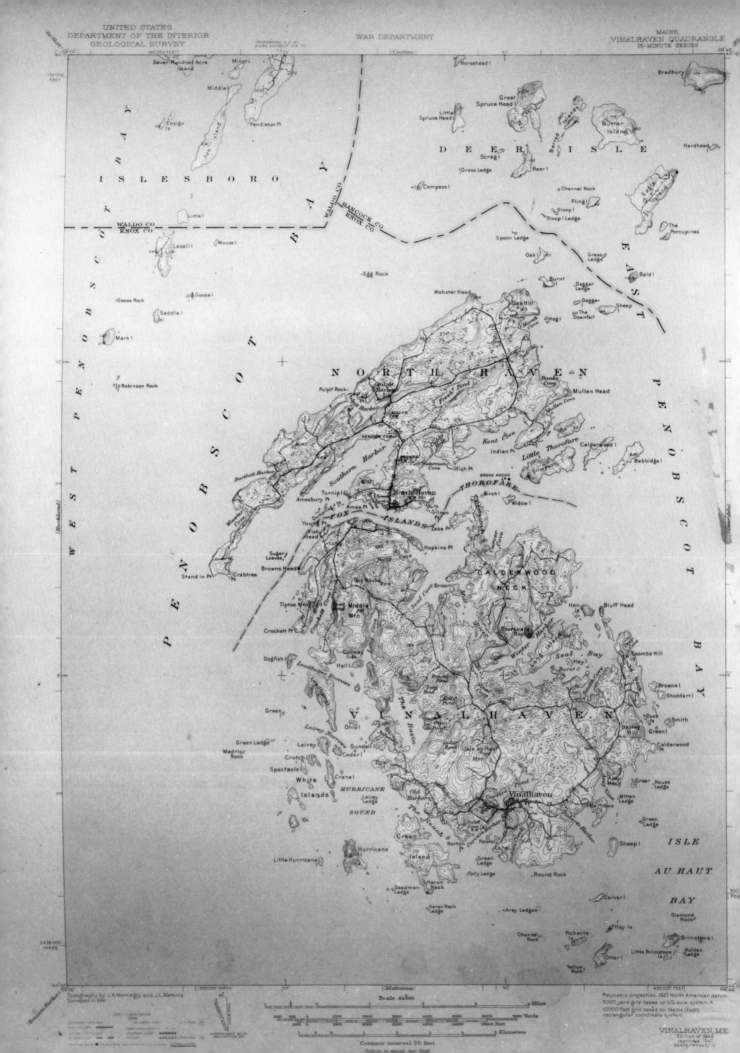

Benson and Maine

by John Wilmerding

When Frank Weston Benson bought the Glover farmhouse on North Haven Island in the early years of the twentieth century, he was following in a long tradition of artists, adventurers and vacationers who journeyed to the Maine coast for inspiration and pleasure. The painters had come for glimpses of a pure and dramatic wilderness, one that, though increasingly settled and populated by the late nineteenth century, still offered to Benson and his contemporaries a special experience of expansive sunlight and water, bold rocky shores and stark stands of evergreen. Benson combined these elements in his most successful paintings—brightly colored, sunfilled depictions of young women and children engaged in a variety of outdoor activities.

Almost every major American painter had visited Maine, briefly or for long sojourns, some to work in quiet privacy, most to record aspects of the region's geography and atmosphere. Among the pioneers in the early nineteenth century were Thomas Birch, Alvan Fisher, Thomas Doughty and Thomas Cole, all of the founding generation of American landscape painting. Birch and Fisher worked for periods in the Boston area. Birch executed a few unidentified coastal views during the 1810s and 1820s, while Fisher traveled as far as Camden and Mount Desert to sketch and paint the distinctive hills in those areas.

In the 1830s, when coastal travel was still arduous, Doughty also sailed as far as Mount Desert. There he painted a memorable image of the lighthouse on isolated Mount Desert rock that was subsequently popularized in a well-known engraved illustration. Cole followed in the 1840s, drawing Mount Desert's bold, narrow fjord, Somes Sound, and painting Otter Cliffs and Frenchman Bay along the island's southeastern shore. These were essentially romantic artists who favored the pictorial language of the sublime, emphasizing man's smallness in the face of the wilderness and the grandeur of nature's forces. Stormy seas and confrontations of rock and water provided them with an heroic language with which they celebrated the American landscape's physical and spiritual powers.

During the 1850s Fitz Hugh Lane began making regular summer trips to the Maine coast, painting views of Portland Harbor, the promontories and coves of southern Penobscot Bay, and the Blue Hill and Mount Desert areas. The Maine summer light, both at midday and at twilight, catalyzed the development of his mature, luminist style. During some of these summers, and continuing into the 1860s, Frederic Edwin Church also traveled to this coast, first following Henry David Thoreau's footsteps into the northern interior, where he painted Mount Katahdin, then remaining close to the southern and eastern coastlines of Mount Desert Island, where he undertook hundreds of pencil and oil sketches. Church's vision was more scientific than that of his predecessors, and his objective eye and meticulous draftsmanship

Opposite:
Map of North Haven and Vinalhaven Islands in Penobscot Bay, Maine.
United States Department of the Interior Geological Survey, War Department, 1947 reprint. Courtesy of Mary and John Brock

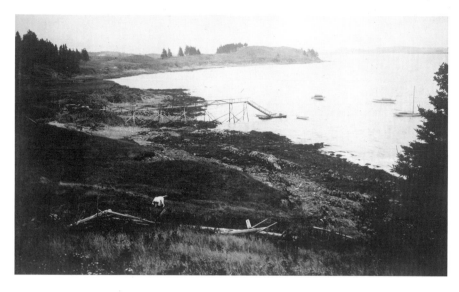

turned especially toward capturing the meteorological nuances of day's most dramatic transitions—sunrise and sunset. We can now see that the hot flares he painted across his canvases were, on a deeper level, signals of the impending national crisis and civil strife at mid-century. In this period the revolutionary thinking of scientists like Charles Darwin would exert its influence on both sides of the Atlantic. In the 1860s and 1870s, while painting the Rhode Island and Massachusetts coastlines, William Stanley Haseltine also made extensive drawing trips to Mount Desert. He sketched and painted the rugged granite outcroppings in works that reveal less a concern with the larger picturesque panorama than the intense, close-up scrutiny of a geologist.

In the last quarter of the nineteenth century, steamship and railroad transportation facilitated travel along the coast, and a general increase in wealth and a decrease in working hours stimulated the growth of leisure and vacation time. Sprawling shingled hotels began to be built in resort regions like Bar Harbor, and summer cottages began to proliferate on many of the beautiful, large islands like Isleboro, North Haven and Vinalhaven in Penobscot Bay. Some artists still made occasional pilgrimages down the coast, even as far as Grand Manan in the southern end of the Bay of Fundy, to record the wild scenery and weather. These were mostly second-generation painters of the Hudson River or luminist schools, such as Alfred Thompson Bricher, William Trost Richards, John Henry Hill, William Hart and Sanford Gifford.

Other powerful stylistic expressions were starting to emerge—for example, the bright palette and mood of American impressionism and the serious, philosophical realism of Winslow Homer, now settled in his family compound at Prout's Neck. The impressionists were of course responding in part to the new artistic developments they were encountering in Europe, but the plein-air method of painting also perfectly suited the comfortable materialism and relaxed vacation habits of Victorian America. In the years around the turn of the century, John Singer Sargent painted during at least one summer on Ironbound Island in Frenchman Bay. Nearby, Childe Hassam did an oil of Green Mountain on Mount Desert viewed from across the bay at Winter Harbor; he also undertook his colorful series of garden views on Appledore Island, further south in the Isles of Shoals. Rocks, light, and water were the shared elements in the works of all these artists, and they would continue to

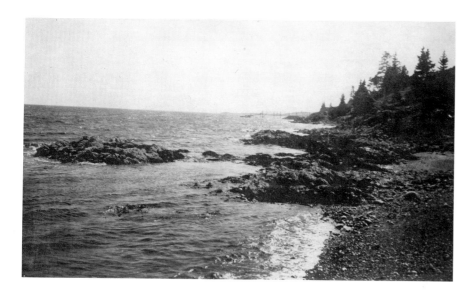

appeal to artists in the twentieth century. We see this in Edward Hopper's stark depictions of the ledges and lighthouses around Portland and in the works of John Marin and Marsden Hartley, who frequently saw these elements as possessing an abstract and expressive character, as in their views from Fox Islands Thorofare and Deer Isle to Schoodic peninsula.

What powerfully attracted artists for more than a century—artists working in different modes of realism, luminism, impressionism and expressionism— was a visually appealing coastline with a striking geography and climate. Maine's rockbound shore of countless islands, inlets and bays was the result of geological activity in prehistory: first, volcanic eruptions and lakes contorted the North Atlantic continental shelf; later, ice-age glaciers ground and gouged the coastal mountain ranges, leaving further shaping to the perpetual erosion of the ocean's tidal forces. The results of all this activity were ranges of hills rising almost from the shore, as at Camden, Blue Hill and Mount Desert, and broad shapely islands like those in Penobscot Bay.

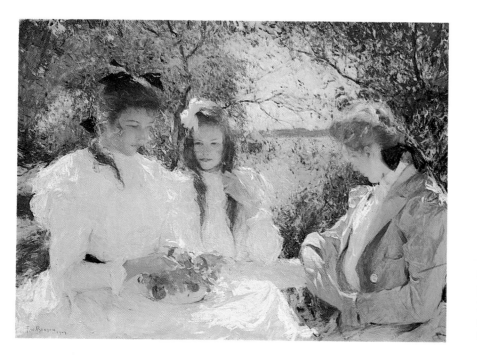

fig. 3
Frank W. Benson, *Portrait of My Daughters,* 1907. Oil on canvas, 26 × 36⅛ inches. Collection of the Worcester Art Museum, Worcester, Massachusetts

One of the most scenic of these is North Haven Island, home to ancient Indian tribes, as many parts of the Maine coast were before the arrival of European settlers. Its waters provided bountiful fishing, and the land yielded timber and granite. By the nineteenth century many of its gentle hillsides and fields were given over to farming. In the decades after the Civil War, vacationers from Boston, New York and Philadelphia purchased and renovated or built frame cottages for summer use. Artists who might have previously visited by steamship or sailboat now came to stay for the season. The painter Beatrice Whitney Van Ness was a good friend of Frank Benson, as were the Boston sculptors Frederick Warren Allen and Bela Pratt. The four, all affiliated with the School of the Museum of Fine Arts in Boston, were summer neighbors on North Haven.

When Benson arrived in the early 1900s, he purchased a farmhouse nearly a century old on Wooster Cove in the island's west district.[1] He decorated its walls with murals showing island views, and over several seasons he produced a body of sun-flooded canvases showing his family basking in the quiet, bright pleasures of the island's summer days. Wooster Farm, as it came to be known, was the setting for many of Benson's paintings (see figs. 1, 2). Situated on a narrow piece of land less than one hundred yards wide, it offered in one direction a spectacular view of the Camden Hills on the mainland and in the other, a panorama of Vinalhaven island. *Portrait of My Daughters* (fig. 3) was painted looking towards Camden, while *Calm Morning* (pl. 4) looks across the Fox Islands Thorofare toward Vinalhaven. The critic Charles H. Caffin, commenting on Benson's summer residence, wrote, "It is a place where life and art can be consistently at one: both partaking freely of the inspiration of the surroundings and working together for good."[2]

Benson's best subjects were members of his family, especially his children Eleanor, George, Elisabeth and Sylvia (see figs. 4, 5). They appear in all of his major outdoor paintings from the turn of the century through the late 1910s. When his children were grown, Benson turned to his grandchildren for inspiration, painting them in his favorite North Haven meadows and hillsides. Both generations are represented in the 1916 painting *Eleanor and Benny* (pl. 12); ten years later Benny appears with his brother Ralph in *Two Boys* (see Dugan, fig. 13), a work in the collection of the Metropolitan Museum of Art, New York. Both canvases were painted at Wooster Farm.

fig. 4
The Benson family on the lawn at Wooster Farm, 1907. From left to right: George, Elisabeth, Ellen, Sylvia, Eleanor and Frank. Photograph. Courtesy of the Essex Institute, Salem, Massachusetts

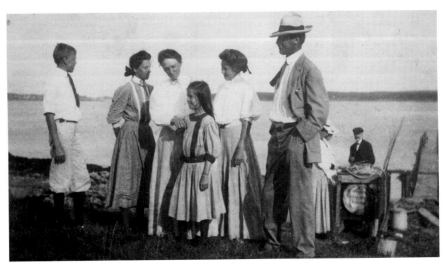

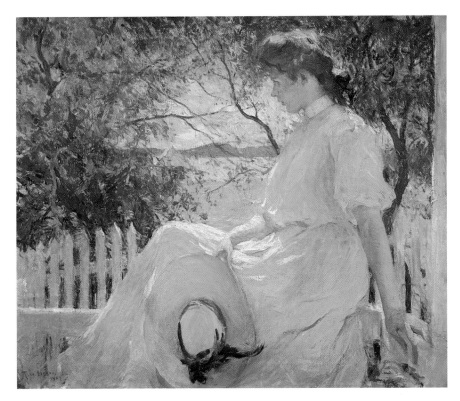

fig. 5
Frank W. Benson, *Eleanor*, 1907. Oil on
canvas, 25 × 30 inches. Collection of the
Museum of Fine Arts, Boston

Although all of his children served as models, Eleanor posed for a number
of outdoor canvases, and of one picture a critic noted, "It is worth the affection
of its being. . . . It is full of the breath of the open world. The artist's insistent
youth is in it, that dower of a man gifted with love of all outdoors."[3] These
paintings of Benson's family were personal works of devotion and celebration.
Usually his sitters posed enjoying simple, fashionable pastimes—fixing a
bowl of flowers, pausing in meadows, watching activities on the water, reading
a book in the shade, idling away the time in small boats. Occasionally, he
dressed a figure in clothing to suggest a mythological personification of
summer, but almost always his young women were bathed in warm sunlight in
pictures with titles suggesting appropriately restful moods: *Calm Morning,
Summer, Evening Light, Sunlight, Afternoon in September.* Impressionism's
bright colors and breezy strokes perfectly matched both the happy mood of
the *belle époque* and the enduring appeal of the Maine atmosphere.

As an American artist Benson is esteemed as a major figure in the so-called
Boston school, an influential teacher at the School of the Museum of Fine Arts,
and an accomplished painter of waterfowl. But it is in his Maine paintings that
we have some of his happiest and strongest work, executed according to his
uncomplicated impressionist principles: "I simply follow the light, where it
comes from, where it goes to."[4]

Footnotes

[1] For a history of North Haven see Norwood P. Beverage, comp., *The North Island: Early Times to
Yesterday* (North Haven, Me.: North Haven Bicentennial Committee, 1976).
[2] Charles H. Caffin, "The Art of Frank W. Benson," *Harper's Monthly Magazine* 119 (June 1909): 111.
[3] Minna C. Smith, "The Work of Frank W. Benson," *International Studio* 35 (October 1908): cii.
[4] Lucien Price, *Frank W. Benson, 1862–1951*, exh. cat. (Salem, Mass.: Essex Institute and Peabody
Museum, 1956), p. 9.

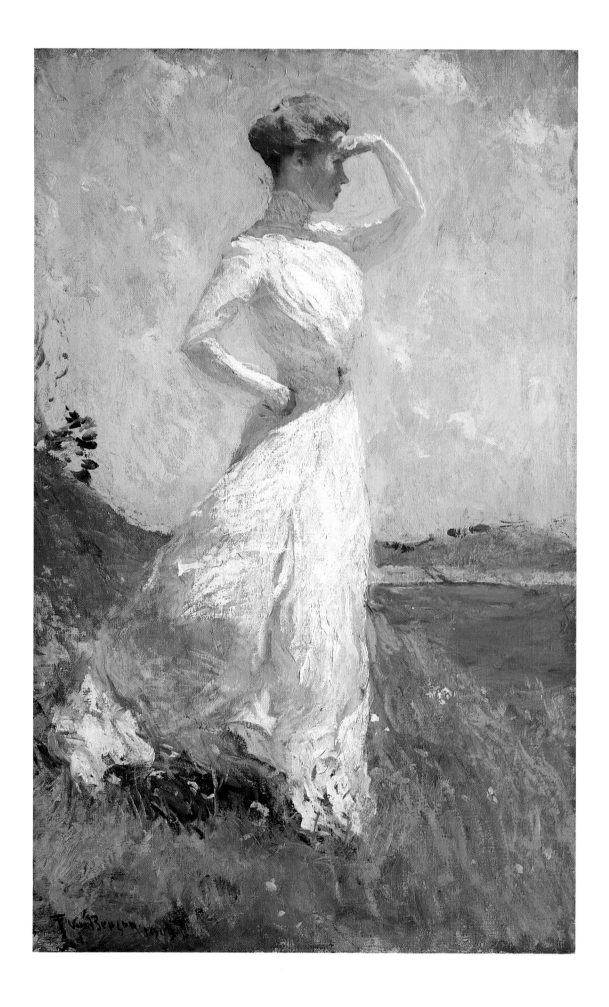

Frank Benson: Outdoors

by Sheila Dugan

Frank W. Benson went to Maine intending to vacation, yet every summer, for over twenty years, he painted several major canvases, creating an extraordinary group of outdoor images. The new setting allowed him to break away from the style he employed during the rest of the year in his Boston studio. Rather than painting figures in dimly lit, decorative interiors, he turned to portraying his subjects—usually his wife, Ellen Peirson Benson, their son George, and their three daughters, Eleanor, Elisabeth and Sylvia—in outdoor light, standing on windy hilltops or beside sparkling blue coastal ranges. He sought to combine the beauties of Maine and of his family on canvas. Occasionally he included family friends in the paintings, but his favorite subjects were his children. They appear in almost every significant outdoor scene painted during the 1900s and 1910s.

Benson bought Wooster Farm, his summer home, in 1901 and continued to vacation there for the rest of his life. Unlike many of the other homes on North Haven Island, which were large, turn-of-the-century "cottages" with guest houses and quarters for servants, the Benson home was modest, built around 1800 as part of a working farm. The large barn, situated a short distance from the house, was used by Benson as a studio. The house provided a welcome retreat, isolated as it was on a large grassy slope. Its charm can be seen in a watercolor which Benson painted in 1927 (fig. 1). Nearby was the apple orchard which provided the setting for several of Benson's most affectionate paintings of his family. Possibly the most attractive feature of Wooster Farm for the children and adults alike, however, was its proximity to the ocean, which was visible from the house and grounds and easily reached in a short stroll.

Benson's images of life at Wooster Farm highlight its idyllic qualities and convey the energy, freedom and playfulness of his youthful subjects. The paintings give no hint of the fog banks that often roll in on summer afternoons or of the damp gray days that seem to last for weeks. When he painted his family, Benson's interest in outdoor light and atmosphere extended only to bright, clear, calm weather. As William Howe Downes wrote, "He sets before us visions of the free life of the open air, with figures of gracious women and lovely children, in a landscape drenched in sweet sunlight, and cooled by refreshing sea breezes."[1]

To express this vision, Benson turned to an impressionist approach, evident in his use of bright colors, gestural brushwork and plein-air subject matter. Impressionism provided him with a vehicle for conveying the beauty of Maine light and the quiet joy of his family's leisure activities, yet he also maintained a carefully structured method and a concern for decorative values that reveal his academic training. To achieve his desired compositional and aesthetic results, the artist also relied on photographs and often repeated

Opposite:
Frank W. Benson, *Sunlight* (see fig. 7)

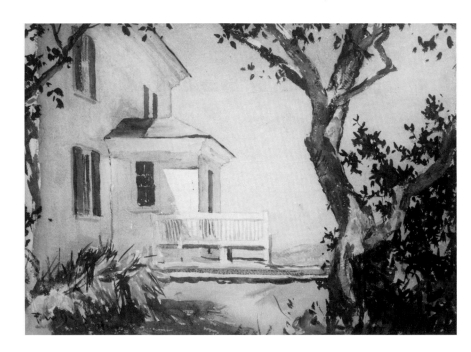

fig. 1
Frank W. Benson, *Wooster Farm*, 1927.
Watercolor on paper, 15 × 21½ inches.
Private Collection

aspects of one work in another. These methods, studied for the first time in this essay, provide new insight into Benson's unique blend of impressionism and an academic manner.

Like many other Boston artists Benson began his career at the School of the Museum of Fine Arts in Boston and then went on to study between 1883 and 1885 at the Académie Julian in Paris, under Gustave Boulanger and Jules-Joseph Lefebvre. In both his domestic training and his studies abroad, he learned sound design and good draftsmanship. These skills became deeply ingrained; despite his exposure to a wide variety of styles, his link with the academic tradition endured throughout his career.[2]

Benson's exposure in Paris to painting styles other than those taught at the academy must have readied him, at least subconsciously, for the impact that French impressionism would have on American art and on his own technique. Although not quite the "prophet of Monet and of Manet" that Minna C. Smith, an enthusiastic critic of Benson's work had dubbed him, he was aware of the new style, as any artist working in Boston in the 1890s would be.[3] Benson was a member of the St. Botolph Club, which in 1892, 1895 and 1899 showed the work of Claude Monet, and of the Copley Society, where ninety-five canvases by Monet were shown in 1905. Benson's membership in the important group The Ten American Painters surely influenced his leanings toward plein-air painting as well. The group included William Merritt Chase, Thomas Wilmer Dewing, Childe Hassam, Willard Metcalf, Robert Reid, Edward Simmons, John H. Twachtman and J. Alden Weir from New York, and Joseph DeCamp, Edmund C. Tarbell and Benson from Boston.[4] The association was formed in reaction to the restrictive policies of the two major artist-organizations of the day, the National Academy of Design and the Society of American Artists, both in New York. Although no particular aesthetic was put forth by The Ten, its members were committed to a freedom of expression and to experimentation rather than an effort at pleasing authorities and winning medals. Although not all members of the group painted in an impressionist style, this tendency was dominant in the works of several, Benson, Tarbell, Twachtman, and Weir most prominently, and Benson was no doubt encouraged by his participation in the group to carry his exploration of the style further.

In 1898, the year in which The Ten held its first exhibition, Benson painted one of his key impressionist works, *Children in the Woods* (pl. 1), which depicts his children Eleanor and George playing in a clearing in the woods. *Children in the Woods* marked a major change in direction not only in subject matter but also in style. Many of the new formal concerns he addresses here— such as an intense interest in light as it envelopes and defines figures in the outdoors, and an emphasis on forms and their placement within the overall context of the design—would appear in his paintings for the next two decades.

Children in the Woods was widely exhibited and received positive reviews. One critic wrote: "Mr. Benson's work portrays delightfully two children at play in the pine woods. The little girl who is dressed in white, might, in less skilful [sic] hands, have become a too aggressive note in this sombre setting, but she seems in truth as much a part of the place as the trees themselves, so admirably is she painted. The lad also takes his place well but without the charm of his playmate."[5] Perhaps in response to this critical success, Benson began to work outdoors on a regular basis. He continued to paint in the more or less impressionistic manner with which he is associated until the mid-1910s when his style became more controlled. By 1909, his outdoor paintings had become familiar to the critics. As Charles Caffin wrote that year: "For as we know him to-day, and have known him for some time, Benson is now preoccupied with the beauty of sunlight in its relation to landscape and to figures disposed in the freedom of the open-air environment."[6]

Benson repeated the subject of children in a forested clearing in a 1905 work also entitled *Children in the Woods* (pl. 5). The painting reveals how far Benson had come in response to impressionism since his earlier rendition of the subject in 1898. Light filters more naturally through the dense evergreens behind the young girls, casting dappled patterns across their pink and white dresses. The girls, seated in a circle, are silhouetted by the dark screen of trees immediately behind. Hair ribbons are tossed playfully by the wind; a comfortable mood of summer leisure permeates the scene.

The subject of figures enjoying the pleasures of outdoor experience had become an important part of Benson's oeuvre by 1903. It was in this year that the artist established a new theme centering around the hilltop motif, for which he is best remembered today. The depiction of a figure or figures, often in profile, at the crest of a hill looking out across the landscape conveys the artist's love of the outdoor life and also of inward reflection. Benson's hilltop images masterfully link the American enjoyment of the openness of this country's landscape with the Boston School preoccupation with introspection and reverie.

One of the best of this genre, *The Hilltop* of 1903 (pl. 3) features the same subjects as in *Children in the Woods* (pl. 1), Eleanor and George (with the addition of the family dog), set against a wide expanse of cloud-filled sky. There is a sense of expectation in the air, a tension created by an unseen focus at sea. Eleanor stands at attention, waving her handkerchief; George shields his eyes from the glaring sun in order to scan the water; even the dog appears rapt in anticipation. Only the ocean-side imagery of Winslow Homer's paint-

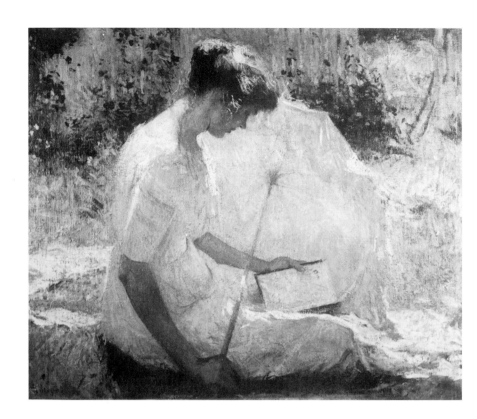

fig. 2
Frank W. Benson, *The Reader—A Summer Idyll*, 1910. Oil on canvas, 25¼ × 30 inches. Private Collection

ings of Long Branch, New Jersey, executed some thirty years earlier, offer any close parallels to Benson's hilltop views. As in Benson's images, Homer's figures are carefully and purposefully posed; they brace themselves against the rushing wind and often seem to anticipate a seafaring visitor.

Stylistically, *The Hilltop* occupies a midway point in Benson's oeuvre. Although some areas of the landscape are painted with the quick rhythmic brushstrokes characteristic of French impressionism, there are patches of heavy impasto, particularly in the clothing. The emphasis on the figures, the flat, smooth brushstrokes and the handling of the light, which is never allowed to dissolve form, show the persistence of his academic training. Yet Benson also exploits the spontaneous qualities occasioned by the scene—the swirls of fabric at the hemline repeat the dancing shapes in the clouds, a flowing waistband and tie flutter toward the sky, and windswept grasses smother the girl's feet—all reminding us of the transitoriness of the setting. The image of a young girl silhouetted against a wide expanse of sky was one to which Benson returned repeatedly. For the next ten years, it was a staple of his outdoor paintings.

In *Calm Morning* (pl. 4), perhaps more than in any of his other paintings, Benson's subject is the intense Maine light and its shimmering reflections on water, but especially its effect on the interior of the boat and on its occupants—Eleanor, Elisabeth and George. In some respects Benson comes even closer here to impressionist precepts, but in other ways he deviates from them considerably. The children are not caught in a fleeting moment of awareness; instead they are carefully positioned—each facing a different direction and patiently awaiting their first bite of the day.[7] The coasting schooners in the scene are not haphazardly plying the waves; they are organized in a way that leads the viewer into a distant, realizable space. Even the all-pervasive light stops short of dissolving the objects—if anything, it emphasizes the solidity of the forms in the picture. Benson passed on to his students this modified approach to impressionism. "Lay the values in flat," he was fond of saying, "The most important parts of a picture are where the edges meet, or one thing comes against another."[8]

Calm Morning was extremely well received. Caffin was including the painting when he noted in 1909: "In these latest pictures of his, children play a beautiful part. He has always been fond of painting them, and naturally feels that they belong to the out-of-door environment; and, what is more, he succeeds in realizing the relationship in his pictures. The children are not merely in the landscape; they are rather an emanation of it, forms in which the sentiment of the scene is focussed and interpreted."[9]

In some ways the outdoor canvases can be viewed as a variation on the interior themes the artist was painting during the 1890s and 1900s. In them Benson took the aesthetic of the Boston School and reinterpreted it in outdoor terms. Caffin also wrote perceptively about this relationship: "[the interiors] were composed with a great regard for decorative effect. . . . The fact is noteworthy as indicative of the process of Benson's development. Consciously or unconsciously he was disciplining hand and eye by close observation and conscientious rendering of the beauty immediately seen against the day when his art should lead him out-of-doors to a wider vision of things."[10]

Two paintings, *Woman with Geraniums* (pl. 8) and *The Reader—A Summer Idyll* (fig. 2), are closely related to Benson's earlier interiors in the use of a single figure totally absorbed in a quiet activity. The decorative quality of these paintings is reinforced by an emphasis on the figure as a structural element in the design. Facial features are vaguely defined, as are details of apparel;

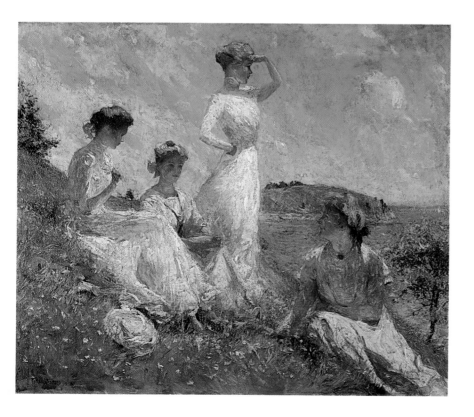

fig. 3
Frank W. Benson, *Summer*, 1909. Oil on canvas, 36⅜ × 44⅜ inches. Collection of the Museum of Art, Rhode Island School of Design, Providence, Bequest of Isaac C. Bates

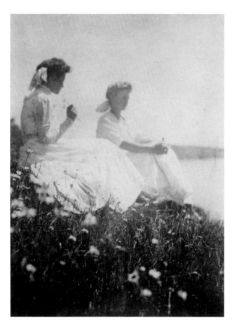

fig. 4
*Elisabeth Benson and Anna Hathaway,
North Haven, Maine,* 1909. Photograph.
Courtesy of the Essex Institute, Salem,
Massachusetts

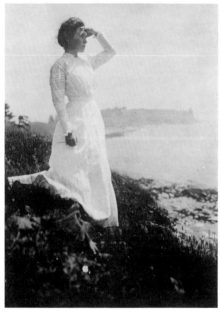

fig. 5
Eleanor Benson, North Haven, Maine, 1909.
Photograph. Courtesy of the Essex Institute,
Salem, Massachusetts

Benson's main intention is one of blending the components of the woman with the surrounding floral environment, in essence establishing her as the main flower among all the others.

Much of the beauty of these works lies in the reserved, pensive nature of the women. We see this same quiet mood in another example, *Eleanor and Benny* (pl. 12), in which the mother sits contemplating her baby. Here the artist contrasts the passive gentleness of the young mother with the more active figure of the child, who is carefully propped up against the pillows on the bench. The bench itself not only acts as a strong design element, but as the linkage between mother and child. The personal and intimate feeling for his subjects that Benson conveyed in his paintings was noticed by reviewers. Leila Mechlin, a noted Washington critic of the period, commented in 1921: "His paintings of figures of women and children out of doors are enchanting—not weakly pretty, but characterful and lovely."[11]

Benson was at his best in the casual outdoor scenes that combine portraiture and genre painting, works such as *Afternoon in September* (pl. 10), *Eleanor and Benny*, and *Summer Day* (pl. 9). The artist depicts members of his family as they relax on the lawn or dock at Wooster Farm, conveying his affection for them and expressing their pleasure in the familial experience. In these refined, genteel paintings the figures never appear remote from the viewer. The psychological distance so obvious in the outdoor figure paintings of Abbott Thayer, Philip Leslie Hale and Thomas Wilmer Dewing is missing in Benson's work. Rather, the women often look as if they have paused momentarily in their everyday activities. The two women in *Afternoon in September* are deeply engrossed—one in her reading, the other in her mending—yet we feel that they have only just returned to their concentrated activities and could at any moment resume a lengthy discussion.

Despite the expansive, open feeling of many of the outdoor canvases, the subjects themselves often appear quite intimate with each other. At times they seem to be engaged in deep conversation; at other times they are absorbed in thought. Reviewers attributed the personal qualities of Benson's paintings to the fact that he was painting his own family, clearly his favorite subject in these exterior scenes. However, Benson also achieves this familiarity through poses and expressions, the way in which the figures interact with one another, and the ease with which they exist within their environment. We sense the strong bond of their shared childhood experience, as in *Summer Day,* where Elisabeth and Sylvia Benson sit on a dock and look out over the water, the scene of so many joyful adventures of their youth.

Laddie (pl. 6), in which the subject is the son of a neighboring family, retains the intimacy that critics liked, but is also strongly decorative. This aspect is enhanced by the flat patterning of the screen of leaves placed behind the child, which also serves to compare the child's young limbs to those of the flowering tree. In *Laddie* as in many of his outdoor portraits of very young children, Benson proves his adeptness at integrating the small figure into the landscape and conveying a sense of intimacy between the subject and nature—and in this case the viewer as well.

With *Portrait of Elisabeth* (pl. 2) the artist returns to the hilltop motif, silhouetting the young girl against a brilliant summer sky. Although Benson's approach is here more reductive than in earlier examples, the painting exhibits the essentials of the hilltop pictures; a figure beautifully enveloped in sunlit skies and ocean breezes.

Despite their individualized features, some critics read Benson's figures as a type. Caffin saw in them an aristocratic nature, comparing them to "something of the character of a fine blooded race-horse, long in its lines, clean cut, spare of flesh, the bone and muscle felt beneath it, movement throughout accentuated . . . a cross between the exacting narrowness of Puritanism and the spiritual sensuousness and freedom of Emerson, a transcendental blend of morals and imagination. . . . By the time I came to understand it, it seemed to me to embody very remarkably the ideals of this country."[12]

Others recognized qualities of traditional portraiture in the work, but astutely noted the modernist tendencies as well. Downes observed in a 1911 issue of *Arts and Decoration* that Benson's "outdoor pictures of his own children combine the human interest of portraiture—an unconventional and intimate sort of portraiture—with an exquisitely complete decorative effect. Nothing could be more perfect than the unity of relationship between the figures and the landscape setting."[13]

Benson's theories of light, color and design were recorded by his daughter Eleanor Benson Lawson in a journal she kept from 1929 to 1949. In it she noted the advice her father gave as she learned to paint. One theme that runs throughout the text is the emphasis on design: "A picture is merely an experiment in design. If the design is pleasing the picture is good, no matter whether composed of objects, still life, figures or birds. Few appreciate that what makes them admire a picture is the design made by the painter."[14] Another time, explaining why things in the distance seen through a mist seem so much more handsome then those seen in clear detail, he commented, "Simply because it allows you to see the design and does not destract [sic] your attention with unimportant small things."[15] On a third occasion he remarked, "You will always get into trouble unless you design all the time you are painting."[16]

Although the decorative elements of Benson's work were noticed by his critics, the extent to which he planned his compositions has never been fully revealed. Reviewers took for granted that Benson painted in the open air. For example, Caffin wrote that "the feature that will stand out with strongest emphasis is the artist's new behavior toward nature: his going out to study it in all its own natural environment of light and his rendering his impressions of it actually in its presence. This, as contrasted with the old idea of making piecemeal notes of nature and then withdrawing with them into the seclusion of the studio to make a more or less arbitrary use of them, will stand out as the essential characteristic of present day painting."[17]

Despite Caffin's claim that all of Benson's summer work was rendered outside, there is ample evidence to suggest otherwise. Photographs depicting the exact subjects of a number of Benson's outdoor paintings indicate that he used the camera in his working process. In addition, a number of canvases present single subjects that are repeated with minor variations in other larger, multiple-figure works. For the purposes of this discussion, these works will be termed "isolated figure" paintings. They are not "studies" in the traditional sense. The artist considered the paintings finished works in their own right,

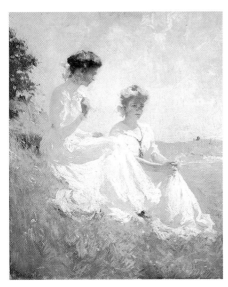

fig. 6
Frank W. Benson, *Elisabeth and Anna*, 1909. Oil on canvas, 32 × 25 inches. Private Collection

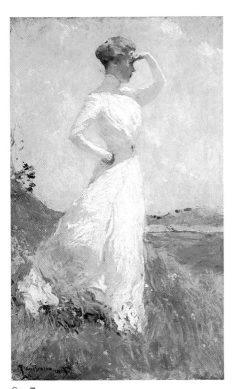

fig. 7
Frank W. Benson, *Sunlight*, 1909. Oil on canvas, 32¼ × 20 inches. Collection of the Indianapolis Museum of Art, John Herron Fund

fig. 8
Frank W. Benson, *On Lookout Hill*, 1914. Oil on canvas, 50 × 65 inches. Collection of the Detroit Athletic Club

signing them and including them in important exhibitions. Photographs and isolated figure paintings enabled Benson to compose his works carefully, especially the larger figural groups which are among his best known today.[18]

Summer (fig. 3) is one of Benson's most thoroughly documented compositions. To produce it, he drew on photographs (figs. 4, 5) and at least two smaller isolated figure paintings: *Elisabeth and Anna* (fig. 6 and pl. 7), which shows the artist's daughter and Anna Hathaway, a family friend, and *Sunlight* (fig. 7), which portrays Eleanor.[19] These two works are closely related to *Summer.* The time of day, figural poses, and light and shade in these are treated almost exactly as they are in the larger painting. However, the two young women in *Elisabeth and Anna* take on a very different importance. They are placed closer to the foreground rather than being set back on the hill, and therefore appear nearer to the viewer. The flowers in the foreground of *Summer* are minimized in *Elisabeth and Anna* increasing our sense of intimacy with the figures. A warm light suffuses the work and the figures seem more at ease than in *Summer.* The standing figure no longer enframes the two-figure group, and this, too, adds to the expansiveness of the imagery. When we compare the photographs with *Elisabeth and Anna* and *Sunlight*, it also becomes apparent that Benson took liberties in rendering his subjects, idealizing them as he transferred them onto canvas—elongating their waistlines, correcting their posture and adding grace to the position of their arms. The photographs may also have contributed to Benson's decorative approach, heightening his tendency to flatten forms—especially those in shadow—strengthen contrasts and crop areas of landscape.

Benson did not leave a record of his exact procedure. We can only surmise that the smaller works were done first and then grouped together, probably in the studio, to form the basis of more complex compositions. Rather than rejecting the method of "making piecemeal notes of nature" commented on by Caffin, Benson seems to have exploited it fully. In fact, his academic training may have directly contributed to his process of combining several different works into a carefully arranged composition. The photographs may have helped him remember the poses after his daughters and their friends had tired of sitting or aided him in other ways to complete the works.

For Benson's *On Lookout Hill* (fig. 8), there are also a number of related works—*The Hill Top* (fig. 9 and pl. 11), *The Hillside* (fig. 10), and a small untitled study in a private collection.[20] It is extremely probable that the large painting was created in several sessions rather than in one plein-air exercise. Standing on a steep hill the figures in *On Lookout Hill* seem more precarious in their placement, and less intimate with each other than those in other works on the hilltop theme. The three are separated spatially from each other and seem lost in individual reflection: one figure reads under an umbrella; another seated figure is caught up in private reverie; and the standing figure, her stately dress curving around her sinuous physique, looks out across the landscape or, probably, the ocean. The central standing figure also appears in the isolated figure painting *The Hill Top*. In this case the smaller work is as striking as the larger one. The clouds which are gathered behind the figure in the larger work are not as tightly clustered in the smaller version, hence the sense of freedom and open space around the figure is stronger in this work. The curves and lines of the figure's arms, hat, and umbrella, which are given full attention in the *The Hill Top*, are easily missed in the multi-figured *On Lookout Hill*.

In some cases the works are even more closely related. This becomes evident when we compare *Summer Day* (fig. 11 and pl. 9) with an unlocated work of the same subject (fig. 12) that also includes an additional figure in the right portion of the canvas. For *Summer Day*, Benson removed this awkward third figure and the dock railing that stands in front of the two seated figures. The results of these changes are immediately apparent. An easy calm pervades

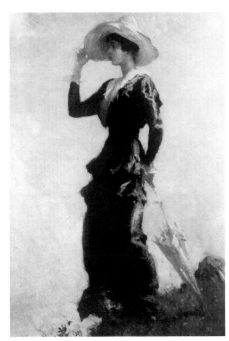

fig. 9
Frank W. Benson, *The Hill Top*, 1914. Oil on canvas, 40 × 32 inches. May Family Collection

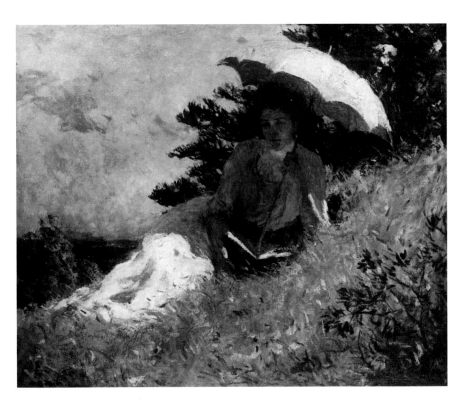

fig. 10
Frank W. Benson, *The Hillside*, 1921. Oil on canvas. Location unknown. Photograph courtesy of the Spanierman Gallery, New York

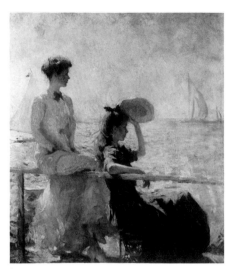

fig. 11
Frank W. Benson, *Summer Day*, 1911. Oil on canvas, 36⅛ × 32⅛ inches. Collection of Mr. and Mrs. Raymond J. Horowitz

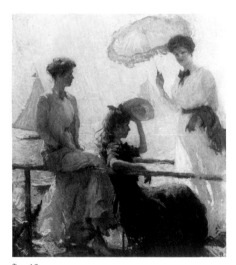

fig. 12
Frank W. Benson, *Elisabeth, Sylvia, and Eleanor*, c. 1911. Oil on canvas. Location unknown. Photograph courtesy of the Society for the Preservation of New England Antiquities, Boston

Summer Day; the two women sit in hushed attention, in awe of the shimmering sea before them. The painting has the feel of an immediate impression, although as the other rendering strongly implies, it was probably a second, perfected treatment of the subject.

That not all of the artist's outdoor scenes were painted *en plein air* is finally confirmed by a letter from one of Benson's grandchildren referring to the painting *Two Boys* (fig. 13). In the letter, he states, "I well remember posing for this picture. . . . We actually posed for a water-color. The oil painting must have been done in his studio from the water-color."[21] This work, which is in a private collection, was painted in 1924; the oil was executed two years later.

Although Benson is almost always categorized as an American impressionist, from 1896 through 1920 his interpretation of impressionism varies considerably, ranging from the more tightly painted works like *Calm Morning* with its broad, flat areas of color, to paintings such as *Evening Light* (fig. 14) which is much closer to French impressionism, with its loose style and figures blended into the landscape. As this work suggests, Benson could have painted in a less formal manner than he usually chose to produce the scintillating effect of a summer evening. Instead, he adopted elements of a plein-air approach while still maintaining his close link to the academic tradition in which he was trained. He confirmed the importance of composition and design in his writings and kept his principles firmly in mind when he worked. The surviving photographs, the many isolated figure paintings, and the reappearance of the same subjects—sometimes in altered form and sometimes in nearly exact repetitions—provide evidence that he drew on many sources to create his outdoor paintings. However, his methods do not detract from the message that his Maine paintings deliver; they remain the quintessential vision of the summer hiatus and the escape from urban pressures to leisurely abandon and timeless August days.

Footnotes

1 William H. Downes, "The Spontaneous Gaiety of Frank W. Benson's Work," *Arts and Decoration* 1 (March 1911): 195.

2 For a discussion of the academic bias in the works of Boston School artists, see chapter VI of Bernice Kramer Leader's *The Boston Lady as a Work of Art: Paintings by the Boston School at the Turn of the Century* (Ann Arbor: University Microfilms International, 1980), Ph.D. dissertation, Columbia University, 1980.

3 Minna C. Smith, "The Work of Frank W. Benson," *International Studio* 35 (October 1908): cii.

4 For a discussion of the Ten American Painters, see Donelson F. Hoopes, *The American Impressionists* (New York: Watson-Guptill, 1972); Richard J. Boyle, *American Impressionism* (Boston: New York Graphic Society, 1974); Kenneth Haley, *The Ten American Painters: Definition and Reassessment* (Ann Arbor: University Microfilms International, 1975), Ph.D. dissertation, State University of New York at Binghamton, 1975; Patricia Jobe Pierce, *The Ten* (North Abington, Mass.: Pierce Galleries, 1976); William H. Gerdts, *American Impressionism* (Seattle: Henry Art Gallery, University of Washington, 1980) and his *American Impressionism* (New York: Abbeville Press, 1984). At Twachtman's death in 1902, Chase joined the group.

5 B. F., "Ten American Artists," *New York Evening Post*, 6 April 1899, p. 7.

6 Charles H. Caffin, "The Art of Frank W. Benson," *Harper's Monthly Magazine* 119 (June 1909): 109.

7 That same summer the artist painted two smaller studies for *Calm Morning*.

8 Eleanor Benson Lawson, "Advice from F. W. B.," typescript, Frank W. Benson Family Manuscript Collection, James Duncan Phillips Library, Essex Institute, Salem, Mass., p. 1.

9 Caffin, "The Art of Frank W. Benson," pp. 112–13.

10 Caffin, "The Art of Frank W. Benson," p. 109.

11 Leila Mechlin, *The Washington Star*, cited in "Benson Exhibition," *Boston Evening Transcript*, 25 March 1921, p. 35.

12 Caffin, "The Art of Frank W. Benson," p. 106.

13 Downes, "The Spontaneous Gaiety of Frank W. Benson's Work," p. 196.

14 Lawson, "Advice from F. W. B.," p. 5.

15 Lawson, "Advice from F. W. B.," p. 6.

16 Lawson, "Advice from F. W. B.," p. 7.

17 Caffin, "The Art of Frank W. Benson," p. 112.

18 The earliest instance of this was in 1899 when the baby in *The Sisters* (Collection of the I.B.M. Corporation) was depicted in an isolated figure painting.

19 A third isolated figure painting entitled *Sunlight Study*, included in Benson's one-man exhibition at the St. Botolph Club in 1910 is now unlocated. At one time it was owned by the artist's friend and neighbor on North Haven, Bela Pratt. A photograph in the Essex Institute identifies the figure as Gretchen Strong.

20 Benson usually completed a large canvas and related works in one summer. The isolated figure painting *The Hillside* is an exception; it was painted seven years after *On Lookout Hill* and *The Hill Top*.

21 Benson's grandson, to Dr. Doreen B. Burke, 13 March 1979, Archives, Department of American Paintings, Metropolitan Museum of Art, New York.

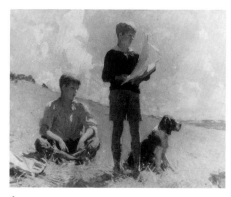

fig. 13
Frank W. Benson, *Two Boys*, 1926. Oil on canvas, 32 1/16 × 40 1/8 inches. Collection of the Metropolitan Museum of Art, New York, George A. Hearn Fund, 1927

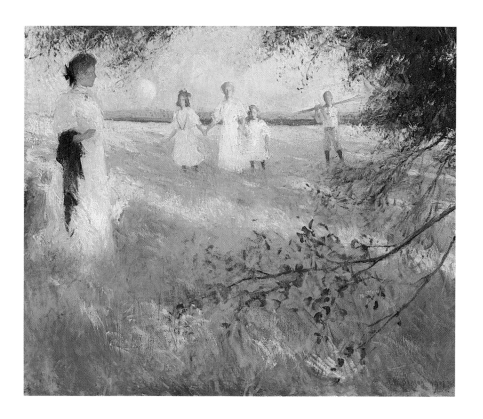

fig. 14
Frank W. Benson, *Evening Light*, 1908. Oil on canvas, 25 1/4 × 30 1/2 inches. Collection of the Cincinnati Art Museum, Kate Banning Fund

27

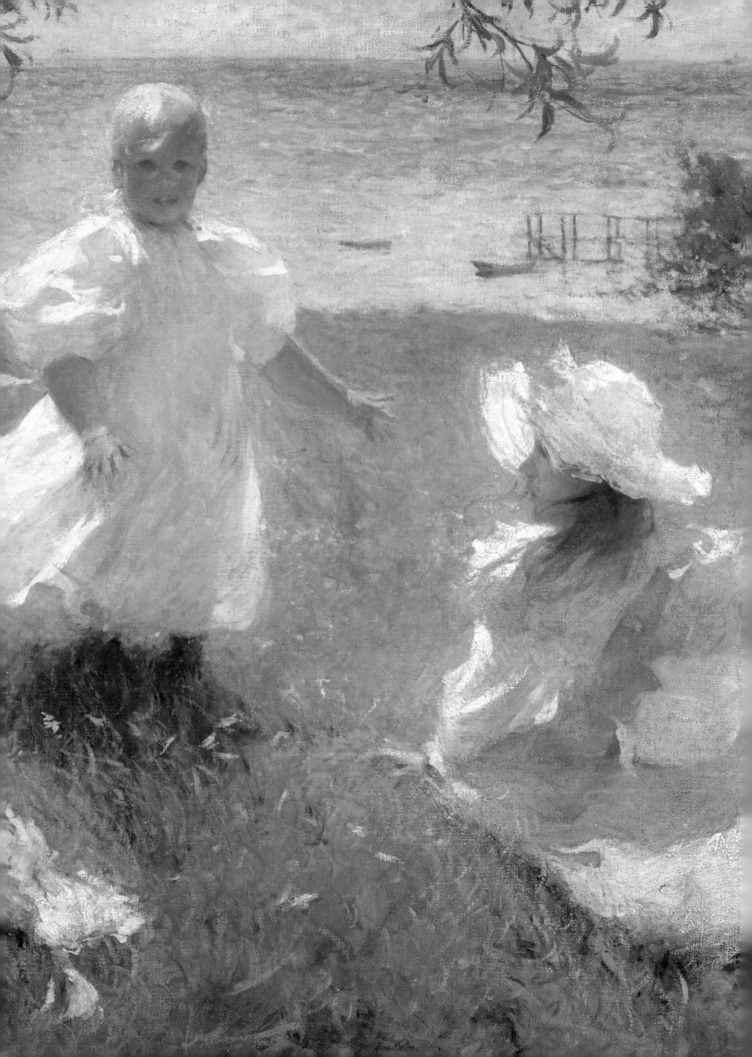

Frank Benson — His Own Man:
A Study of the Artist's Development and Its Critical Reception

by William H. Gerdts

The present exhibition consists of a group of superb and characteristic examples by Frank Benson, one of the acknowledged leaders of the "Boston School," the group of painters at least loosely identified with that regional manifestation of impressionism at the turn of the century. These distinctive and distinguished artists were and have continued to be recognized as figure painting specialists, despite their occasional forays into other genres, including not only the allied field of portraiture but also still-life and landscape painting. An historical conundrum that yet remains to be explained is why this identification was so firmly established and ingrained, despite the fact that impressionist works by local landscape artists such as Theodore Wendel and John Leslie Breck appeared in public exhibitions in Boston earlier than did examples by the figure painters Edmund Tarbell and Frank Benson. But this paradox is not the topic here under discussion.

What does need to be considered is the development of the role that Frank Benson played and established as his own within the homogeneous aesthetic of the Boston School. Often Benson is and has been viewed as one of a group of almost indistinguishable though extremely talented painters that includes, in addition to Tarbell, William Paxton, Joseph DeCamp, Philip Hale and countless others, some of whom remain less well identified, at least so far. In a sense, their reputations suffer not only from this narrow identification, but also from their ascription as followers of Tarbell. And conversely, Tarbell's art has had to sustain charges of so easily engendering imitation.

Indeed, the detrimental nature of this allegation of aesthetic homogeneity early assumed a concrete and specific designation: the artists were deemed "Tarbellites," named, of course, after Edmund Tarbell. Such an appellation implied both Tarbell's primacy in the evolution of their shared aesthetic and the dependency of the remaining artists of the group upon his achievements. It acknowledged Tarbell as an innovator and relegated the others, including Benson, to the secondary rank of imitators. As we shall see in exploring Benson's early maturity, the case here is far less simple and clear, for although Benson and Tarbell did share analogous artistic goals and explored similar aesthetic problems, they often did so at different times and with differing intensity and longevity of commitment.

It was the extremely perceptive critic Sadakichi Hartmann who appears to have originated the term "Tarbellite"; in fact, in *Art News*, one of the several insightful if short-lived periodicals that Hartmann founded and for which he was a primary writer, he published an article in 1897 entitled "The Tarbellites."[1] He noted that this was a name he had himself coined for a certain set of Boston painters who had lately become conspicuous. He identified the leader of the group based on his impression that:

Opposite:
Frank W. Benson, *The Sisters*, detail (see fig. 9)

It is impossible to stay for any length of time in Boston and be interested in art matters without hearing of Tarbell. Rumors are afloat about him stating that he is one of the greatest painters living, and, mind, not only of America but of the world. . . . Let us enter one of their exhibitions. There are lamp and firelight effects, and an occasional lawn fete. There are mothers with children, sitting in a boat, on the piazza, or in an orchard, and who apparently have no interest in life, except a mania for posing in sunlight. The Tarbellites are also very fond of depicting models, some-times nude, but generally dressed up like society girls. . . . Tarbell's picture lacks just what might save it—individuality.

For the most amusing quality of the Tarbellites is that one can never be sure which of them painted this or that picture. This year de Camp [sic] exhibits a picture that seems to be technically a facsimile of Benson's picture of last year, and next year Benson will come forth with a canvas that will look like a Tarbell of several years ago. Individuality is deemed unnecessary, and now and then a mild character actor like Phillip [sic] Hale appears amongst them. In order to become a Tarbellite one must merely manage to cover large surfaces with pyrotechnic displays of technique. This is why the school has so many followers.

Had Hartmann's discussion remained embedded in this original ephemeral publication, the term and its implications might well have been ignored, but he repeated his statements, almost verbatim, in his influential two volume work, *A History of American Art*, published in 1902. Here he noted the European prototypes of the style of these painters, pointing out that "still more palpable in contemporary art are those accomplishments of our young painters which were derived from the innovations of Degas, Raffaelli, Besnard, Zorn, Boldini, etc. They are best expressed in the work of the Tarbellites, a clan of Boston artists under the leadership of E. C. Tarbell (1862–). . . . To repeat, nature is their motto, which is very meritorious to say the least; yet one shortcoming is attached to it: if two or three painters paint the same subject, and they invariably do, it becomes very difficult to decide about the authorship."[2]

Hartmann's pronouncement "took" in critical art circles and remained the dominant mode of interpretation for over three decades. It was promulgated again in an influential analysis of the Boston painters by the prestigious artist-writer Guy Pène du Bois in 1915. In his essay du Bois contrasted the Boston artists with the Pennsylvania landscape school, which centered around Ed-ward Redfield and his work. He found the distinction clear-cut in subject, style and philosophical purpose: the Pennsylvania men were democratic, forceful landscape painters, whereas the Boston artists were elitist figure painters. And he identified Tarbell as "the real leader of this group," which embraced refinement, polite truths, timidity, exclusivity and beauty.[3]

Even Philip Hale, the most articulate of all the members of the Boston School, acknowledged Tarbell's supremacy and his regional identification, writing that "Most of the artists of this country will, if you say 'Boston' to them, reply 'Tarbell.'"[4] And more recently, Beatrice Kramer Leader, in her important and incisive dissertation and the several articles that she has drawn from it, has discussed the Boston artists as a school whose work has a unified sociological as well as aesthetic identity. Thus once again in critical and scholarly opinion, Tarbell assumes the artistic lead, although other painters, especially William Paxton, defined most conclusively the conservative attitudes toward the hermetic and passive role of upperclass Boston women, a subject that Leader treats as well.[5]

Yet even Leader excepts Benson to some degree from the common characterization of the Boston School style—in her dissertation, by noting his artistic dissimilarities from the group, and in her articles, by his limited appearance within her discussions. And so might he well be removed from beneath the Tarbellite umbrella, though he was, in fact, the artist most closely allied with Tarbell both professionally and personally of all the group. While it is true, as Leader has carefully recorded, that they both studied at the School of the Museum of Fine Arts in Boston with the same instructors and then went abroad to Paris to continue their artistic training at the Académie Julian, their careers were not entirely parallel. Tarbell entered the Museum School in 1879 and Benson a year later; Benson went to Paris in 1883, and Tarbell did not go abroad until 1884. Benson was at the artists' colony in Concarneau in the summer of 1884 and in November was in London, whereas Tarbell's European travel was more extensive—to Germany and Italy, in particular, Venice. Even their initial public exhibitions were divergent: Benson's Concarneau scene *After the Storm* was exhibited at the Royal Academy in London in 1885, and Tarbell's *La Lecture* was shown at the Paris Salon the following year.

Although the careers of the two artists did not immediately converge on their return to Boston—Tarbell stayed there but Benson went to his native town of Salem, which remained his residence throughout his career, and was the first teacher at the newly formed Portland Society of Art Drawing School founded in 1886—their lives soon began to show similar patterns. Once back in this country, both artists began to establish their professional identities, initially with portraiture, and began exhibiting at the Boston Art Club— Benson in 1886 and Tarbell in 1887. The following year they both married. Their closest association came when they were appointed to the faculty of the Museum School in 1889, Benson teaching the antique class and Tarbell, painting. They remained on the staff of the school until 1912, and thus the homogeneity of the Boston aesthetic was passed on by the team of Tarbell and Benson for a generation (along with Philip Hale, who joined them in 1893 to teach drawing from the antique, while Benson took over the life drawing class).[6]

Equally important for their growing association was their appearance together, not only in the local exhibitions of the Boston Art Club, but elsewhere in Boston and beyond. Benson first exhibited one of his Concarneau pictures at the Pennsylvania Academy in 1887, but more important to critical perception of his work was his visibility the next year in New York, with *In Summer* shown at the Society of American Artists and *Storm*, presumably his Royal Academy entry of two years before, marking his first appearance at the National Academy of Design. For the next decade, until he joined the newly formed the Ten American Painters late in 1897 and began to show with them faithfully beginning in the next year. Benson's work was regularly seen at the annuals of both major New York exhibiting organizations, as well as in an ever-widening range of national presentations in New England and the Midwest.

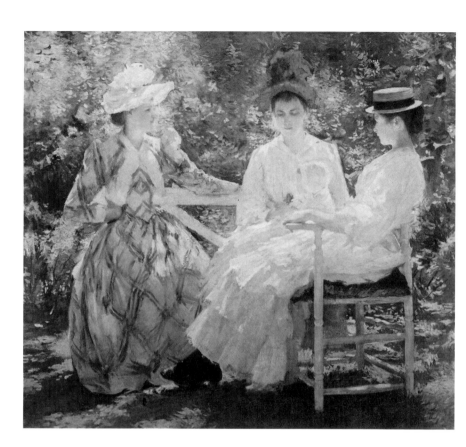

fig. 1
Edmund C. Tarbell, *Three Sisters—A Study in June Sunlight*, 1890. Oil on canvas, 35⅛ × 40⅛ inches. Collection of Milwaukee Art Center, Gift of Mrs. Montgomery Sears

Tarbell's work was on public view earlier in New York than Benson's, for he began exhibiting regularly at the Society of American Artists in 1887, but until 1891 all of the paintings he showed were portraits, while most of his more poetic figure-pieces were displayed during these years at the National Academy, where Tarbell began exhibiting in 1888. The artistic alliance of Tarbell and Benson was confirmed in their two-man exhibition held at the J. Eastman Chase Gallery in Boston in 1891. They were similarly united forty-seven years later in a two-artist show at the Museum of Fine Arts in Boston, which turned out to be a memorial exhibition for Tarbell, and most recently at the University of New Hampshire Art Galleries in 1979.[7]

Despite the charges of uniformity directed at the art of the various members of the Boston School, distinctions between the painting of Tarbell and Benson have been noted. They suggest sometimes simplistically that Tarbell first came to public notice with his colorful outdoor figure-pieces in the 1890s, while Benson's painting was much more subdued during this decade. Only at the end of the 1890s did Benson "move outdoors," according to most scholars, whereas shortly thereafter, under the influence of Vermeer, Tarbell redirected his art toward a much quieter, more refined and conservative presentation of primarily passive imagery of women indoors, in which he was joined by his Boston colleagues, Benson only partially included. The preceding is the summation art historians of the last decade have made, the present author among them.[8]

However, this interpretation is not completely correct, and the development of the two artists and the interaction between their work was, in fact, more complex. While it is customary to imply that Tarbell achieved critical approval before Benson, particularly with his outdoor paintings—initially with *Three Sisters—A Study in June Sunlight* (fig. 1) of 1890, and then with the even more successful *In the Orchard* (fig. 2) of the following year—it was actually Benson who was the first to move away from his concentration on portraiture and enter the arena of the then avant-garde out-of-doors impressionism, with his now-unlocated *In Summer* of 1887 or 1888.[9] Nor did this work go unnoticed or unacclaimed.

In Summer debuted at the annual exhibition of the Boston Art Club in January of 1888 and then became Benson's first picture to be displayed in New York, at the Society of American Artists. The painting was greeted with tremendous enthusiasm by the New York press, partly on its own merits and partly due to the appearance of a new and fresh talent among the ranks of the modern artists. The critic for the *Art Amateur* found "Frank W. Benson treating, rather more successfully than usual, the old problem of a white dress in shadow with a broad stretch of sun-lit lawn for a background."[10] And the writer in the *New-York Daily Tribune* noted that "Mr. B. [sic] W. Benson's outdoor portrait of a young lady in white, with a sunny, green field beyond and a garden in the background, may safely be numbered among the brilliant things of the exhibition, and this exhibition of delicate perception, firmness and self-control in expression stamps the new-comer as a painter of much promise."[11] The critique that appeared in the *New York Evening Post* was quoted in its entirety in the *Nation*. The writer described *In Summer* as a large picture, hung in the middle of the gallery. "This, too, is an out-of-doors subject, a portrait of a young lady in a white dress, who is seen sitting in the shadow on a lawn, which in the middle distance is flooded with sunlight, and extends to a background of trees, and houses, and garden walls beyond. It is very simply

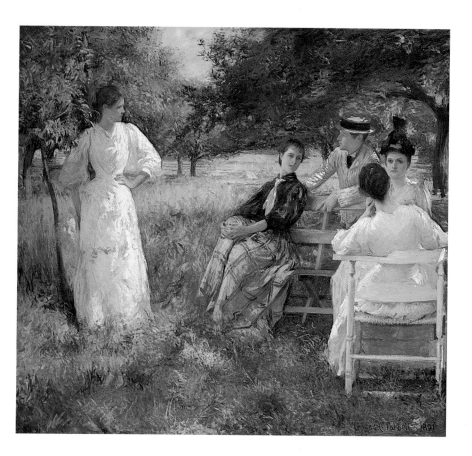

fig. 2
Edmund C. Tarbell, *In the Orchard*, 1891.
Oil on canvas, 60½ × 65 inches. Private Collection

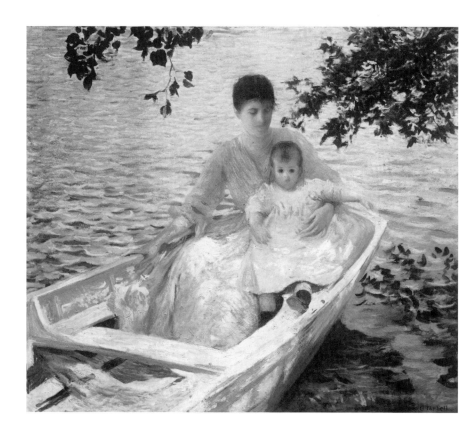

fig. 3
Edmund C. Tarbell, *Mother and Child in a Boat*, 1892. Oil on canvas, 30 × 35 inches. Collection of the Museum of Fine Arts, Boston, Bequest of David P. Kimball in memory of his wife, Clara Bertram Kimball

painted—too simply at times, for it amounts to a positive thinness in certain passages—but it is a remarkably faithful study of values, it is clean and fresh in color, and very good in ensemble. It is to be especially noted as the work of a young Boston artist who has not exhibited before in New York, and who may be safely set down as a painter of whom much may be expected."[12]

The prediction of the newcomer's promise was a major theme in Clarence Cook's review of Benson's work in the *Studio*. Cook devoted a whole paragraph to the picture, commenting that he had previously seen at least one of Benson's paintings in Boston. But he noted: "The artist has boldly burnt his ships and thrown away every chance of retreat by looking at his difficult subject in the broadest way, and allowing himself as little detail as possible . . . and there is enough good workmanship in the picture to make us sure of hearing from Mr. Benson in time to come."[13]

Rarely would Benson again enjoy such enthusiastic and unmitigated praise for his work among the New York critics. *In Summer* went on to represent him in the art exhibition of the 1889 Paris International Exposition, to which Tarbell sent only a portrait. However, in the following year Tarbell enjoyed his own share of acclaim, as his *After the Ball* was displayed at the National Academy of Design in New York and won the Thomas B. Clarke prize for the best American figure composition. This work was a sensitive indoor rendering of a seated young woman seen in the reflection of glowing firelight.

The praise garnered by *After the Ball* was subsequently overshadowed by the renown reaped by the artist's successive outdoor works—the aforementioned *Three Sisters—A Study in June Sunlight*, shown at the National Academy of Design in 1891, and the less well known *A Girl in a Striped Gown—Study in September Sunlight*, which appeared at the same time as *Three Sisters* at the Society of American Artists and was then critically regarded as its companion piece. And Tarbell reinforced his association with colorful outdoor figure-painting by exhibiting *In the Orchard* of 1891 and *Mother and Child in a Boat* of 1892 (fig. 3) at the National Academy annuals of 1892 and 1893, respectively. Nor did he abandon major indoor figural-compositions with an emphasis upon lamplight and firelight effects—*The Opal* (fig. 4), in particular, shown at the Society of American Artists in 1891, elicited as much comment as his earlier *After the Ball.*

What seems presently inexplicable, however, is that after their respective successes with *In Summer* and *After the Ball*, Benson and Tarbell subsequently concentrated upon and achieved renown with a series of compositions emphasizing the distinctive features of each other's first important triumphs. While Tarbell's reputation was enhanced with his series of outdoor scenes, and while Benson did not, of course, totally abandon the outdoors—he even painted a number of attractive pure landscapes during the 1890s—his major and most successful efforts of the early 1890s were lamplight and firelight pictures. He did not seriously return to naturalistic outdoor painting until his *Children in the Woods* (pl. 1) of 1898, the work that announced the new direction his art was to take.

It is no wonder, therefore, that the critics of the nineties confused the two artists and tended to group them together, particularly after they exhibited jointly at the Chase Gallery in Boston in 1891. In that show, both displayed a number of portraits, and in addition, Tarbell's *Opal* was on view. But also seen there were his sunlight pictures, *June* and *September*, and Benson's *Moonlight* and *Twilight*. The latter of this pair was noted in the *Boston Evening Transcript* as similar to Tarbell's *Opal*, "lighted by lamplight, filtered through the same red shade, and producing the same Mephistophelean effect." The writer further found that "These young and talented painters are so much in sympathy with each other that their exhibition has the homogeneity if not the monotony of a collection by one man. Their work is so similar in intention, taste and character that it may be estimated *en bloc*."[14]

The other critics, including the *Boston Post's* eminent Desmond Fitzgerald, a champion of Monet and the impressionists, commented favorably on the exhibition, whereas the reviewer for the *Boston Herald* noted that "the two artists are well mated in this collection, sympathetic in individuality and similar in tendencies . . . [these] Boston painters take exceptional delight in color problems, particularly in studies of light under various conditions; both have a strong feeling for graceful form and a corresponding capacity to give it expression."[15]

From 1890 on, New York critics also tended to group Tarbell and Benson together in their reviews, even when the works were, in fact, aesthetically quite dissimilar, and when they might express satisfaction with the efforts of one and distaste for the other's. For instance, in 1891 the reviewer for the American edition of the English *Magazine of Art* presented a long diatribe against Tarbell's *The Opal* and followed it immediately with a critique of Benson's *Portrait of a Young Girl* that was a good deal less harsh.[16]

But by 1891 Benson was forging a reputation for his studies of lovely young women seen indoors by artificial illumination. In that year the reviewer of the National Academy annual, writing in the *Art Amateur*, noted that Benson's *Twilight* (fig. 5), "with the yellow reflection from the half-concealed

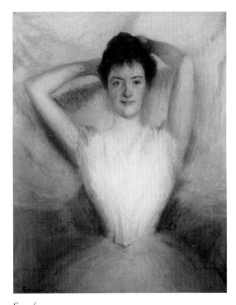

fig. 4
Edmund C. Tarbell, *The Opal*, 1891. Oil on canvas. Private Collection

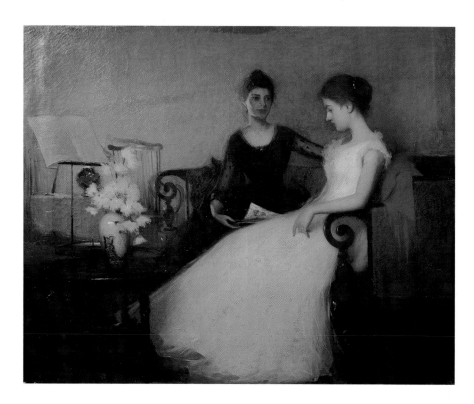

lamp upon the beautiful forms of two ladies, one in white, the other in black, who are exchanging confidences, is one of the best pictures in the exhibition; well composed, carefully drawn and cleverly studied for color." After which he wrote of Tarbell's even greater success with his outdoor painting *Three Sisters—A Study in June Sunlight*.[17]

In 1892 Benson showed *By Firelight*, a picture of a slender woman in black seated before a fire, at the Academy annual; it was greeted by the writer in *Magazine of Art* as a "very nice contribution in his familiar line."[18] The critic for the *New York Sun*, too admired *By Firelight* as an "exceedingly clever study in illumination, like his treatment of lamplight last year. . . ."[19] And Clarence Cook, in the *Studio*, after praising Tarbell's *In the Orchard*, noted that "Next in value to this picture is Mr. Frank W. Benson's 'By Firelight' in the South Room; a picture rich in feeling and with just enough, and not too much of that artificial lighting sometimes too dangerously experimented with by this artist even whose failures have been interesting."[20]

Benson continued to exhibit variations on his chosen theme at the National Academy—*Lamplight—Study in Red, Black and Gold* in 1893 and *By Firelight* in 1894—though they were not always met with the enthusiasm that his earlier examples had elicited (see fig. 6). In 1893, for instance, the writer in the *Magazine of Art* found Benson's picture lacking in grace and compositional unity, but he also noted, perceptively, that "Edmund C. Tarbell of Boston is always bracketed with Mr. Benson, although their methods are very different."[21]

In addition, Benson was exhibiting his firelight and lamplight pictures beyond Boston and New York with increasing frequency. He had begun displaying his paintings in Chicago as early as 1889, when his *Orpheus* was shown at the annual Inter-State Exhibition. Both he and Tarbell were represented at the Columbian Exposition of 1893 with three works each. Benson, characteristically, displayed low-keyed paintings such as *Girl in Red Shawl*, which had previously been seen at the Inter-State in 1890, while Tarbell drew special attention with his colorful impressionist scene, *In the Orchard*. Benson's *Twilight* appeared in the annual American show at the Art Institute of Chicago in 1891 and at the Pennsylvania Academy in Philadelphia the following year, along with *Lamplight*. In 1894 *Lamplight* brought Benson further notoriety when it won a prize at the new art gallery of the Jordan, Marsh & Company department store in Boston. Also that year *By Firelight* was seen at the Chicago annual and as far away as the Nebraska Art Association; it would also appear in 1895 in the annual show of the Cleveland Art Association.

When *By Firelight* was exhibited in Chicago, it elicited one of the most extensive reviews ever devoted to a painting by Benson, in the published three-way conversation among the members of the "Critical Triumvirate"— which consisted of the renowned novelist Hamlin Garland (who was also a patron of Benson), the city's leading sculptor, Lorado Taft, and Charles Francis

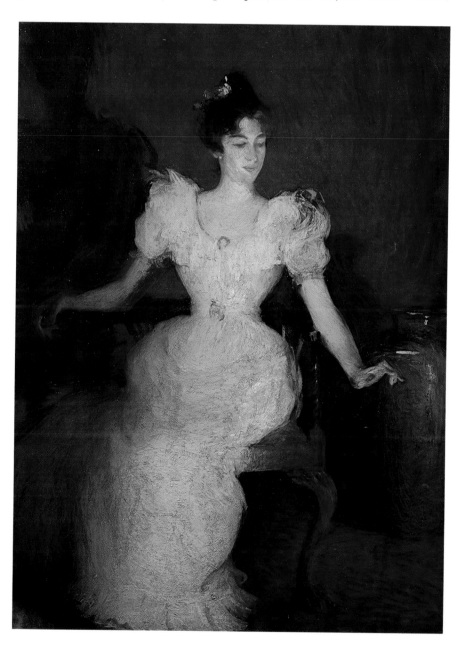

fig. 6
Frank W. Benson, *Firelight*, 1893. Oil on canvas, 40 × 30 inches. Private Collection. Photograph courtesy of the Spanierman Gallery, New York

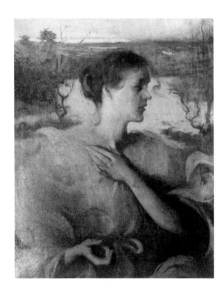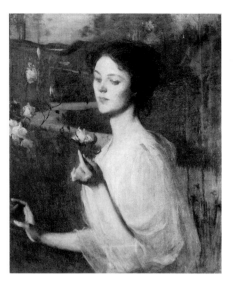

Browne, a well known conservative landscape painter working in Chicago in the Barbizon mode. They reviewed the Chicago presentation in the booklet *Impressions on Impressionism*:

> Novelist [Garland]: Ah! There's Benson's picture, way over there in the corner. I saw that at the Academy of Design. It is masterly. I don't know of anything finer in the way of firelight. See the simplicity of his method. That hand and arm is painted with the broad strokes of the brush, but it takes genius to do that. I think that picture superior to Tarbell's "Arrangement of Pink and Gray."
>
> Sculptor [Taft]: (Before Benson's picture) Isn't she a beauty? How aristocratic and inconspicuous! You told me of her the other day, but I did not dream of anything so crisp and pure in color. Look at those mellow shadows. Do you see the fluffiness of that drapery, the firmness of the flesh—the hardness of that glazed jar—why, man, that thing has all of Zorn's magic with the best American refinement to boot—. . . . See how it is done! See your effect of firelight now. Look at that arm. A stripe of pure vermillion and then next to it one of clean, vivid blue, and then this mass of transparent shadow. You step back three steps and they blend into the tenderest gradations, but preserve a purity that you don't see once a year in a painting. Yes, that is equal to Zorn at his best, and you know how I raved over him last summer.
>
> Conservative Painter [Browne]: Steady—steady now hold up a bit. Benson is a good painter and a splendid fellow as well, but don't put on your praises as some of us put on paint, in chunks. I don't find it so tremendously interesting. In color it is delicate, especially in the shade parts, but I don't believe he needs to fill her hands with vermillion and cadmium to represent fire reflection. The quantity of paint is objectionable, for it's noticeable at the focus distance of the picture; same with yellow on dress—it's too painty. The picture is good of course in its way, but I wouldn't get on my knees to it.[22]

Despite the fascination evinced for his firelight and lamplight pictures, during the next few years Benson's art took a very different turn and again received critical approbation. In this body of work he moved away from bold experimentation with indoor light and, indeed, away from a realist basis, toward more purely decorative considerations. It is a direction that finds no analogue in Tarbell's painting of the same period. Perhaps the artist felt he had carried his study of striking indoor lighting-effects as far as he could. However, we also know that his new concern with the decorative stemmed from his involvement with the mural-decoration program for the new Library of Congress building. In the mid-1890s he contributed to this program two series of mural paintings, one depicting the Three Graces and the other the Four Seasons. In keeping with his previous practice, Benson presented these mythological characters in the form of lovely young women, but they are also more idealized. This approach derived, at least in part, from his friendship with Abbott Thayer and the inspiration provided by Thayer's own painting.

Benson's artistic kinship with Thayer had, in fact, been noted before: when in 1891 his *Portrait of a Young Girl* was exhibited at the Society of American Artists, the critic for the *New York Herald* pointed out that "Frank W. Benson has a capital and decidedly Thayer-like portrait of a young girl in rose seated."[23] And the reviewer for the *Boston Post*, writing on the two-artist show of Benson's and Tarbell's work held at the Chase Gallery in 1891, noted that "Mr. Benson's work shows a hearty liking for that of Mr. Abbott Thayer. . . . Always conscientious and true, he has now learned the poet's license of painting."[24] Much later Benson was to acknowledge his debt to Thayer in a letter to Thayer's widow: "What he was to me in my early years is not to be expressed by any words—without doubt he helped me more than any other influence in the world and the help he gave me is continuing in its effect today."[25]

The results of both Thayer's influence and Benson's involvement with mural painting were immediately apparent when in 1895 he exhibited his *Autumn and Spring* (fig. 7) at the Society of American Artists; they became still more evident the following year when the work was shown in Chicago and Philadelphia. At the Art Institute of Chicago annual, it was entitled *Autumn, Spring, Two Decorative Panels in One Frame*, and at the Pennsylvania Academy it was described as *Decorative Panels, Autumn and Spring. Study for Panels in Congressional Library.*

The New York press was unequivocally enthusiastic; Benson had not received such rave reviews since *In Summer* was shown back in 1888. The writer for the *New York Times* described the work as "full of great charm in idea, execution and sentiment. His picture is a diptych, each panel representing a charming young woman, with appropriate background of the season. A steady advance is noticeable each year in the exhibit of this artist, and the work under discussion is painted with increased freedom, with greater apparent ease, and with a more artistic realization of the unities. Nothing jars, the work is unctuous and full of grace."[26] And the writer for the *Herald* was aware of the source of the new aesthetic: "Frank W. Benson seems to have come strongly under the influence of A. H. Thayer in his two life size half lengths in one frame, representing 'Autumn' and 'Spring.' Even Mr. Thayer's mannerisms in brush work are reproduced in these two works, in which the landscapes and the figures are equally charming."[27]

Benson's new direction received further approval when his *Decorative Figure—Summer* (fig. 8) won the significant Shaw prize of $1500 at the

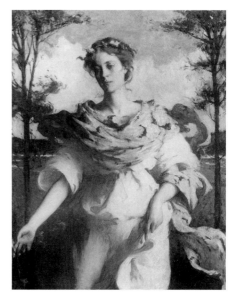

fig. 8

Frank W. Benson, *Summer*, 1890. Oil on canvas, 50⅛ × 40 inches. Collection of the National Museum of American Art, Smithsonian Institution, Gift of John Gellatly

Society of American Artists in 1896. The writer in the *Art Amateur* praised the artist for his ability to express motion by means of line and for his very modern treatment of color and light. And again Benson was allied to his mentor: "He and Mr. Thayer have long constituted one of the many little groups into which our artists seem naturally to fall. They have both been noted for their preoccupation about tone and indifference to modelling. If the habit of working together and learning from one another continues we shall doubtless have within a few years that distinctively American school so much desired by certain critics. But perhaps they will not like it when they get it."[28]

The most fulsome appreciation of Benson's *Decorative Figure*, published in the *Art Interchange*, noted its kinship with a much admired Old Master source: ". . . a notable achievement that recalls Botticelli in its exquisite grace of movement and delightful color scheme. . . . It places Mr. Benson in the front rank of our painters, and reveals his possession of a graceful sentiment with which he had not been credited heretofore. For those who place great value on such matters it may be remarked that the brush work is broad and free, and full of character. While painting in a high key, as was befitting the subject, he has not adopted the extravagance of color or crudeness of manipulation, which characterize many of the luminists, but has turned to the technique of the great painters of earlier times. His methods are both scientific and interesting, but the charm of the work lies in its imagination, its grace, its originality."[29]

It is difficult to estimate the continuing degree of Thayer's influence upon Benson's later work, for by the end of the decade, the artist had assumed a new and, by and large, permanent stance. Since this development appears to have coincided with the formation of The Ten and the group's identification as the core of the impressionist movement in America, Benson's turn to vibrant, colorful outdoor-painting must surely be related to his membership in this organization. That he was named among The Ten, and so an impressionist, is confirmed in an article that appeared in the *New York Times* in 1901. Here the author sarcastically created a subdivision of the "Sacred Ten" called the "Vibratory Seven," which included Childe Hassam, Robert Reid, J. Alden Weir, John Twachtman, Tarbell, and Benson, and excluded Edward Simmons, Thomas Dewing and Willard Metcalf, although the last was soon to be identified among the impressionists also.[30]

Actually, Benson's initial showing in the first exhibition of The Ten, which featured his popular *Twilight*, only reinforced his reputation for low-keyed interiors. However, later that year he emerged fully into the out-of-doors genre with his *Children in the Woods*, shown at the prestigious Carnegie International in Pittsburgh. This painting marked Benson's debut into the pictorial world of outdoor impressionism, and it went on to be displayed internationally. In 1899 it was shown at the second annual exhibition of The Ten, the Art Institute of Chicago, the Cincinnati Art Museum's annual exhibition of American art, the Pennsylvania Academy of the Fine Arts and the St. Louis Exposition and Music Hall Association. In 1900 it was one of the two works representing Benson at the Paris International Exposition.

Though Benson was now, in fact, returning to the outdoor settings with which he had first attracted notice in 1888, among them, *In Summer*, the critics were initially somewhat skeptical. The writer in the *New York Sun*, for

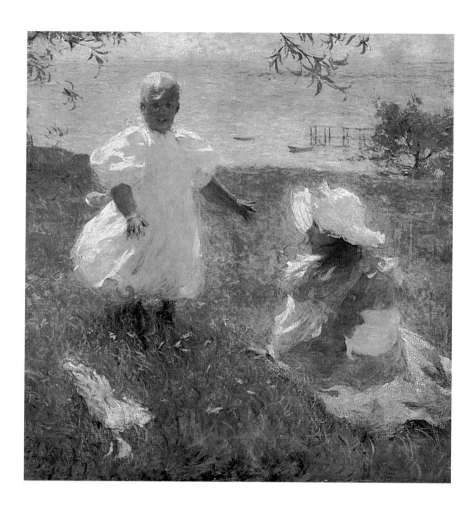

fig. 9
Frank W. Benson, *The Sisters*, 1899. Oil on
canvas, 40 × 39½ inches. Collection of
I.B.M. Corporation, Armonk, New York

instance, reviewing the display of The Ten, found that "Mr. Benson's picture of
a boy and girl in a woods is much more ambitious [than Tarbell's] and it may be
accepted that it was the best thing he had to send, though he has shown much
work that is more sympathetic."[31] Obviously this critic had been more taken
with Benson's earlier firelight and lamplight paintings and Thayer-like decorative murals.

With his 1898 *Children in the Woods*, Benson established both the aesthetic and the motif with which he would become primarily associated for
many years. He further developed these in 1899 in *The Sisters* (fig. 9) which,
like *Children*, he exhibited first at the Carnegie International in Pittsburgh that
year. In place of the more careful figural modeling and somewhat subdued
palette of *Children in the Woods*, in *The Sisters* Benson asserted a new vigor in
his brushwork and employed a riot of color and brilliant whites to depict this
scene set in full sunlight. In terms of palette and handling, this canvas heralds
the artist's work of the following decade.

The Sisters joined *Children in the Woods* to represent Benson in the Paris
International Exposition of 1900, where it garnered him a silver medal, and
the following year the picture was shown at the Pan-American Exposition in
Buffalo as well as in the annual show of The Ten. It had also been among the
works featured in the 1900 retrospective of Benson's art at the St. Botolph Club
in Boston, where it was regarded as his outstanding achievement. The critics
appear to have recognized that with these visions or radiant childhood set in
full outdoor sunlight, Benson had truly come into his own. The writer for the

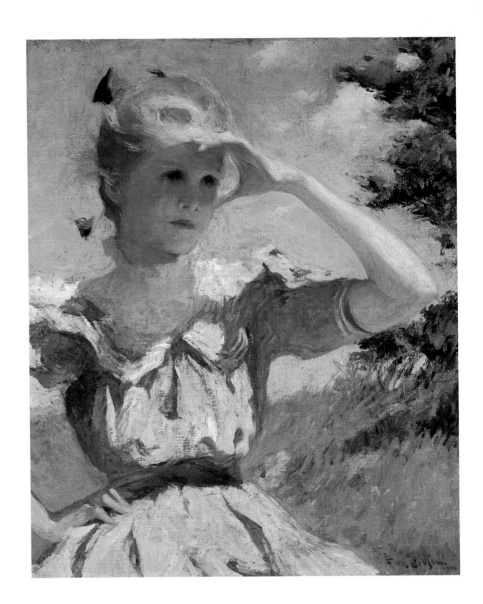

fig. 10
Frank W. Benson, *Eleanor*, 1901. Oil on canvas, 29½ × 25 inches. Collection of the Museum of Art, Rhode Island School of Design, Providence, Gift of the Estate of Mrs. Gustav Radeke

Boston Evening Transcript noted the "ideally blithe vision of youth and summer sunlight. . . . To this blossoming of his art has Mr. Benson worked steadfastly through his career; and as we look back we can trace with ease the successive steps that led in a logical order from the beginnings up to 'The Sisters.'"[32]

The Sisters was no less admired in New York when it was on view with The Ten in 1901. The writer for the *New York Times* observed that "Mr. Benson's Paris picture which took a silver medal was rightly honored. The baby standing in the sunlight on autumnal grass against a background of sea, with a little girl seated near, is a thoroughly successful and beautiful attempt to paint in the open. The flesh painting is luminous, the sunlight strong and true, the attitudes of the children natural, and the coloring delightful."[33] The critic for the *Tribune* found the work "painted with capital animation . . . full of sunshine, skillfully distributed."[34] And the reviewer for the *Sun* remarked: "What a relief it is to turn to Frank W. Benson's 'Sisters,' two little children playing in a meadow by the sea! These are veritably children: healthy, natural types, spontaneously represented; fresh, happy, lovable. What a joyousness of sunshine, and buoyancy of racing air; how invigorating the free play of brushwork and purity of color and, as well, the knowledge and subtle craftsmanship displayed!"[35]

Benson followed *Children in the Woods* and *The Sisters* with a series of masterly outdoor paintings of children, which were continually greeted with great critical acclaim: *Eleanor* of 1901 (fig. 10), *Sylvia* and *The Sea Shell* (alternatively *Child and the Seashell, Young Girl with a Sea Shell, Eleanor Holding a Shell*) of 1902 (fig. 11), and *The Hilltop* of 1903 (pl. 3). *The Hilltop* was an especially honored work, winning a gold medal at the Louisiana Purchase Exposition in St. Louis in 1904 and becoming the first purchase made from the Converse Fund, by the Malden Public Library.[36] Occasionally, when Benson also exhibited indoor subjects, such as his *Portrait of a Girl* shown with *Eleanor* at the annual presentation of The Ten in 1902, the critics expressed admiration for his outdoor paintings but dismissed the interiors.[37]

A further factor in Benson's turn to high-keyed, outdoor figural painting was his acquisition of a summer home, on the Maine island of North Haven, in 1901. There his models were his three lovely young daughters, Elisabeth, Eleanor and Sylvia, and his son George, all of whom matured from infants, to children, to young adults in Benson's images of them. In North Haven, Benson and his family could enjoy first-hand the beauty of unspoiled nature and a landscape setting that was totally compatible with the loveliness of the young children. The countryside also offered the openness, the cool breezes and the warm, flooding sunlight that were so integral a component of the artist's outdoor aesthetic. Maine was perhaps not decisive in redirecting Benson's art—he had, after all, previously painted outdoor scenes, for the most part near Ogunquit, Maine, where the family regularly summered before settling in North Haven. But certainly the substantial increase of such paintings in his oeuvre, their unified character and the importance they assumed in the critical assessment and appreciation of his achievements, suggest that the sympathetic environment he had found was of considerable significance.

By 1905, when Tarbell had turned to the exploration of subtle interior lighting effects derived from the example of Vermeer, the distinction between the two artists was complete. Among the works Tarbell exhibited in New York with The Ten during the organization's early years, *On Bos'n's Hill* of 1901 (titled *Bosse's Hill* when the show was transferred to the St. Botolph Club in Boston) was Tarbell's last major fully impressionist outdoor picture, with the possible exception of *A Summer Breeze*, shown in 1905. That year, the writer in the *Art Bulletin* (after commenting on Tarbell's *Rehearsal in the Studio* and at greater length on his *Girl Crocheting*, which he compared to the paintings of Vermeer) noted that "of Benson's three sunlight pictures, the largest, 'Calm Morning,' [pl. 4] is the most satisfactory, showing a boat with three children, well composed, full of light with excellent atmosphere and distance."[38]

As a reviewer for the *Boston Evening Transcript* noted in 1908, "This is unquestionably Mr. Benson's forte, the painting of figures out in the open. No one achieves such a sensation of a flood of warm, golden light, such an impression of vibrating atmosphere, such a feeling of freedom, joy and wholesome stimulation of vitality."[39]

By now the critics were making clear distinctions between the two artists. While Minna Smith, an early writer on Benson, might note that "Benson and Tarbell came home from Paris, prophets of Monet and Manet," by 1909, James

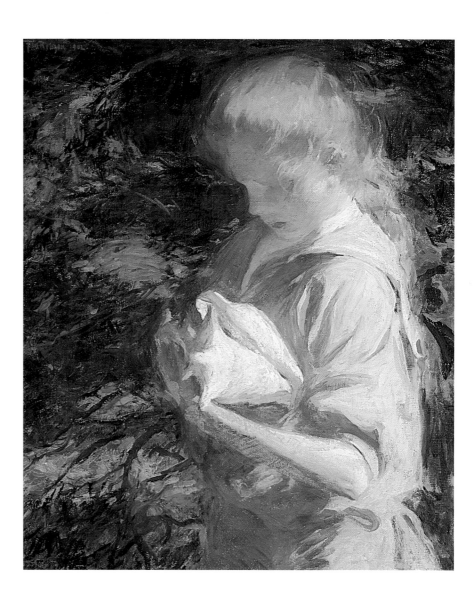

fig. 11
Frank W. Benson, *Eleanor Holding a Shell*.
Oil on canvas, 30¼ × 25 inches. Private
Collection. Photograph, courtesy of the R.H.
Love Galleries, Chicago

Hunneker, in his *New York Sun* review of the exhibition of The Ten, described
Benson as a lover of the outdoors but referred to Tarbell with "the Vermeer
gambit."[40] That same year, Charles Caffin, who, like Smith, was one of the
earliest authors to write specifically about Benson, astutely pinpointed the
diversity of the development of the two artists: "[Benson's] progression repre-
sents a direct opposite to the development of another New England artist,
Edmund Tarbell, whose work I recently reviewed in these pages. With him the
broader outlook came first. The passage of his art has been a gradually closer
and more intimate interest in the subjects of his study. Nor do I make the
comparison invidiously. The real point of interest is that each painter has
faithfully followed the beckoning of his own temperament as it gradually
became plain to him. . . ."[41]

Two years later one of Boston's foremost critics and writers on the city's
art, William Howe Downes, noted that "it is Benson's contributions which
have given the greatest pleasure . . . in comparison with Tarbell's interiors his
outdoor effects are more unlike anything that we recall in European art, more
racy of our soil, and with a more distinctly modern note."[42] And in 1921 Lorinda
Munson Bryant pointed out that: "Although Frank W. Benson, Edmund C.

Tarbell and Robert Reid studied together in Paris at the Julian Academy and also under Dannat, they are entirely dissimilar in their manner of work. . . . In fact, individuality is the dominant note in their paintings. Mr. Benson's brush has caught a certain brightness of colour and light that speaks a language of its own. No one could mistake his manner of entangling the sunlight in the hair and garments of his open air figures. He plays them in the early morning light, and as the evening shadows fall he follows them in the open field and on the hilltop, under sunshades and in open verandas, ever catching the varying quality of sunlight with unerring artistic instinct."[43] Royal Cortissoz, writing in 1936, was even more succinct: "Tarbell had serenity and Benson vivacity."[44]

When in 1938 Benson and Tarbell had their two-artist exhibition at the Museum of Fine Arts in Boston, Loring Holmes Dodd wrote a review in which he described their long association, both personal and professional; he concluded however, that "Tarbell's fine art looks backward, and Benson's is amazingly abreast of its day. Tarbell is a seeker of sunlight in his pictures, it is Benson who really captures it."[45] No better summation of Benson's unique achievements, of those qualities that came to mark his art as distinctly his own, can be found than the description offered in the *Boston Transcript* in 1915: "Sunshiny summer scenes in the big glorious outdoor world, with graceful summer girls in their crisp white frocks, their golden hair blowing in the breeze. . . ."[46]

Footnotes

[1] Sadikichi Hartmann, "The Tarbellites," *Art News* 1 (March 1897): 3–4.

[2] Sadakichi Hartmann, *A History of American Art*, vol. 2 (1901; reprint ed., Boston: L. C. Page and Co., 1902), pp. 237–241.

[3] Guy Pène du Bois, "The Boston Group of Painters: An Essay on Nationalism in Art," *Arts and Decoration* 5 (October 1915): 457–460.

[4] Philip L. Hale, "Painting and Etching," in *Fifty Years of Boston* (Boston: Boston Tercentenary Committee, 1932), p. 357.

[5] See the following by Bernice Kramer Leader: *The Boston Lady as a Work of Art: Paintings by the Boston School at the Turn of the Century* (Ann Arbor: University Microfilms International, 1980), Ph.D. dissertation, Columbia University, 1980; "The Boston School and Vermeer," *Arts Magazine* 55 (November 1980): 172–176; "Anti-Feminism in the Paintings of the Boston School," *Arts Magazine* 56 (January 1982): 112–119.

[6] The best study of the Museum School is H. Winthrop Pierce, *The History of the School of the Museum of Fine Arts, Boston, 1877–1927* (Boston: Museum of Fine Arts, 1930).

[7] See Susan Faxon Olney, *Two American Impressionists: Frank W. Benson and Edmund C. Tarbell*, exh. cat. (Durham, N.H.: University of New Hampshire Art Galleries, 1979).

[8] See Bernice Kramer Leader, *The Boston Lady*, p. 258; Susan Faxon Olney, *Two American Impressionists*, pp. 12–14; William H. Gerdts, *American Impressionism* (New York: Abbeville Press, 1984), p. 214.

[9] Since *In Summer* was first exhibited at the Boston Art Club on January 14, 1888, and was, presumably, begun if not completed the previous summer, as the title implies, it was most likely a work of 1887.

[10] "The American Artists' Exhibition," *Art Amateur* 18 (May 1888): 130.

[11] "Society of American Artists," *New York Daily Tribune*, 18 April 1888, p. 6.

[12] "Society of American Artists," *New York Evening Post*, 28 April 1888, p. 5; "The Society of American Artists," *Nation* 46 (3 May 1888): 373.

[13] [Clarence Cook], "The Society of American Artists," *Studio*, n.s. 3 (May 1888): 95.

[14] "The Fine Arts: Exhibition of Pictures by Messrs. Benson and Tarbell," *Boston Evening Transcript*, 4 March 1891, p. 4.

15 "The Fine Arts," *Boston Herald*, 8 March 1891, p. 12.

16 "Monthly Record of American Art: The Society's Exhibition, New York," *Magazine of Art* 14 (June 1891): xxvi.

17 "The Academy," *Art Amateur* 24 (May 1891): 145.

18 "Monthly Record of American Art," *Magazine of Art* 15 (June 1892): xxiii.

19 "The Academy of Design," *New York Sun*, 9 April 1892, p. 6.

20 "The Sixty-Seventh Annual Exhibition of the National Academy of Design in New York," *Studio* 7 (2 April 1892): 163.

21 "Monthly Record of American Art," *Magazine of Art* 16 (June 1893): xxi.

22 Hamlin Garland, Lorado Taft and Charles Francis Browne, "A Critical Triumvirate," in *Impressions on Impressionism* (Chicago: Central Art Association), pp. 10–11.

23 "Splendid Art Show by the Society," *New York Herald*, 25 April 1891, p. 6.

24 "Some Remarkable Pictures," *Boston Post*, 9 March 1891, p. 14.

25 Frank Weston Benson to Mrs. Thayer, 5 November 1915, Abbott H. Thayer Papers, Archives of American Art, Smithsonian Institution, Washington, D.C., roll D200, frame 910. Originally cited in Susan Faxon Olney, *Two American Impressionists*, pp. 12–14.

26 "The Society of American Artists," *New York Times*, 23 March 1895, p. 4.

27 "American Artists' Attractive Show," *New York Herald*, 23 March 1895, p. 9.

28 "The Society of American Artists," *Art Amateur* 34 (May 1896): 129–130.

29 "The Society of American Artists," *Art Interchange* 36 (May 1896): 16.

30 "The Ten Bolters," *New York Times*, 19 March 1901, p. 9.

31 "Art Notes," *New York Sun*, 6 April 1899, p. 6.

32 "The Fine Arts: Mr. Benson's Exhibition at the St. Botolph Club," *Boston Evening Transcript*, 13 January 1900, p. 15.

33 "The Ten Bolters," p. 9.

34 "Art Exhibitions," *New York Tribune*, 21 March 1901, p. 6.

35 "Around the Galleries," *New York Sun*, 20 March 1901, p. 6.

36 "Benson's 'The Hilltop' Bought by the Malden Public Library," *Boston Evening Transcript*, 1909, clipping (date incomplete), Frank Benson File, Ball Artists Clipping File, Fine Arts Dept., Boston Public Library.

37 "Art Exhibitions," *New York Tribune*, 2 April 1902, p. 9.

38 "Ten American Painters," *Art Bulletin* 4 (25 March 1905): 6.

39 "The Fine Arts: Mr. Benson's Prize Picture," *Boston Evening Transcript*, 9 April 1908, p. 11.

40 See Minna C. Smith, "The Work of Frank W. Benson," *International Studio* 35 (October 1908): cii; James Hunneker, "Nine American Painters," *New York Sun*, 19 March 1909, p. 6.

41 Charles H. Caffin, "The Art of Frank W. Benson," *Harper's Monthly Magazine* 119 (June 1909): 109.

42 See William Howe Downes, "The Spontaneous Gaiety of Frank Benson's Work," *Arts and Decoration* 1 (March 1911): 196–197.

43 Lorinda Munson Bryant, *American Pictures and Their Painters* (New York: John Lane Co., 1921), pp. 182–183.

44 Samuel Isham, *The History of American Painting, with Supplemental Chapters by Royal Cortissoz* rev. ed. (New York: Macmillan Company, 1936), p. 573.

45 Loring Holmes Dodd, "Tarbell-Benson Exhibit Shows Art That Lives," unsourced newspaper clipping, Frank Benson File, Boston Public Library.

46 "Benson's Best Show Exhilarating Outdoor and Indoor," *Boston Evening Transcript*, 9 February 1915, p. 3.

Plates

Plate 1

Children in the Woods

1898. Oil on canvas
40 × 40½ inches
Signed lower left: *Frank W. Benson*
Private Collection

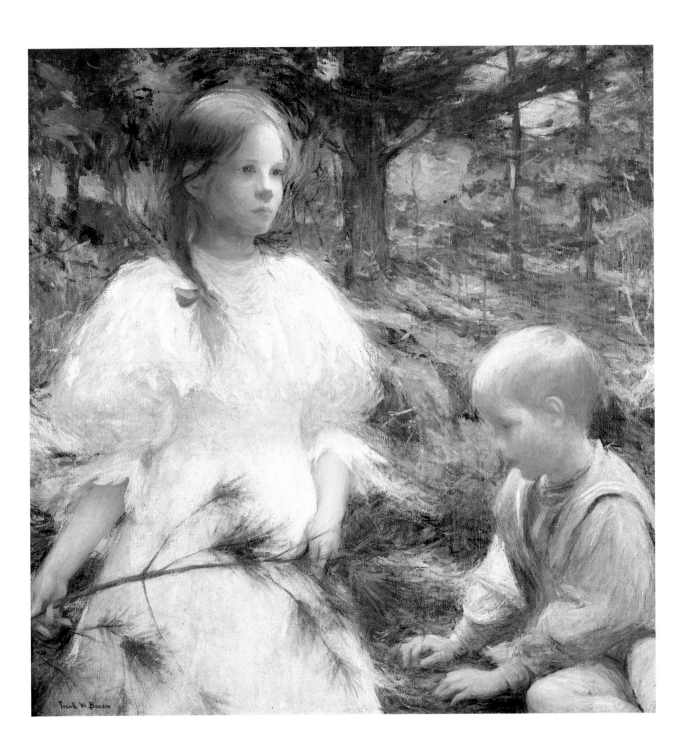

Plate 2

Portrait of Elisabeth

c. 1901. Oil on canvas
30 × 24 inches
Signed (twice) lower left: *F. W. Benson*
Private Collection

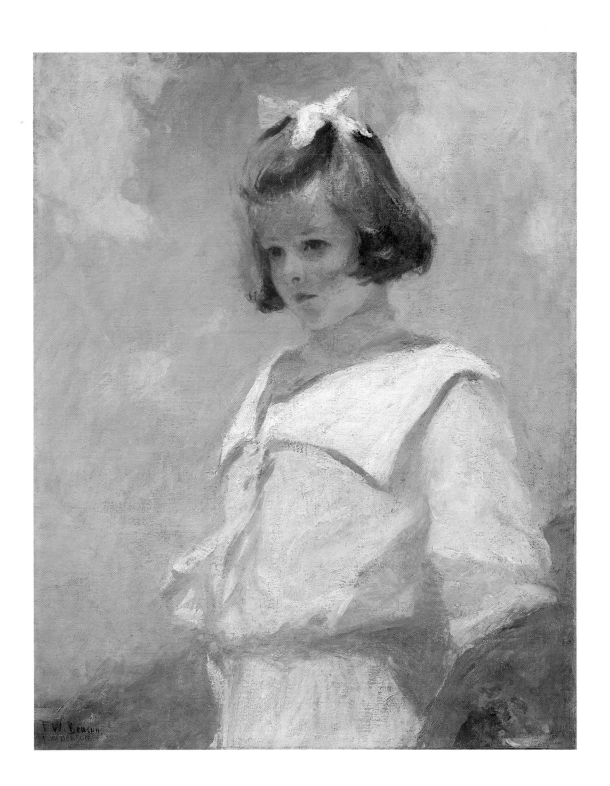

Plate 3

The Hilltop

1903. Oil on canvas
71 × 51 inches
Signed lower left: *F. W. Benson 1903*
Collection of the Malden Public Library,
Malden, Massachusetts

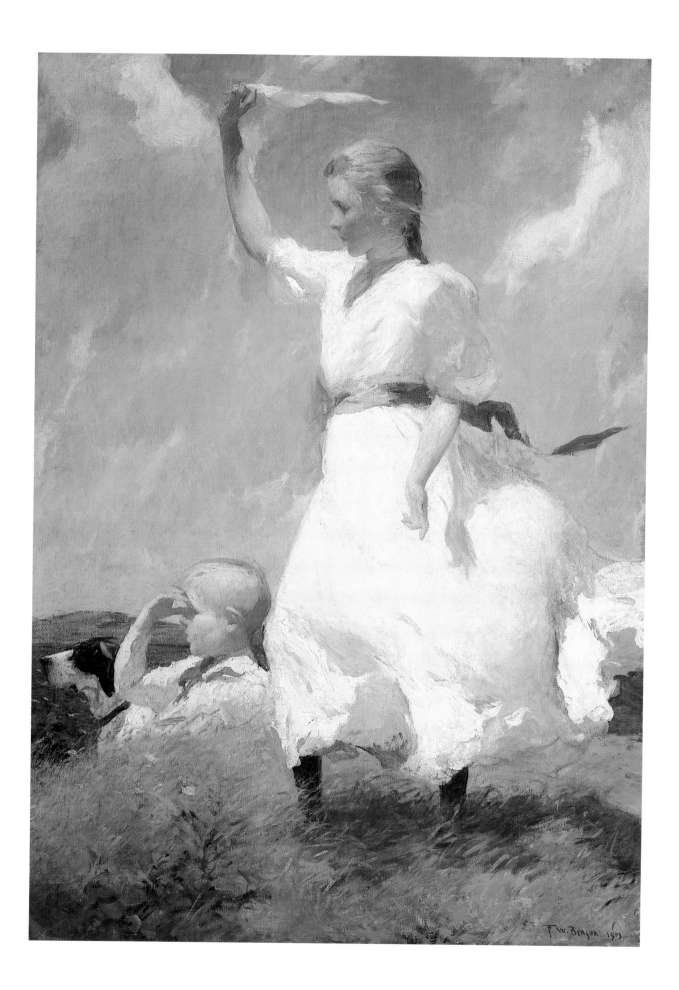

Plate 4

Calm Morning

1904. Oil on canvas
44 × 36 inches
Collection of the Museum of Fine Arts,
Boston, Gift of the Charles A. Coolidge Family

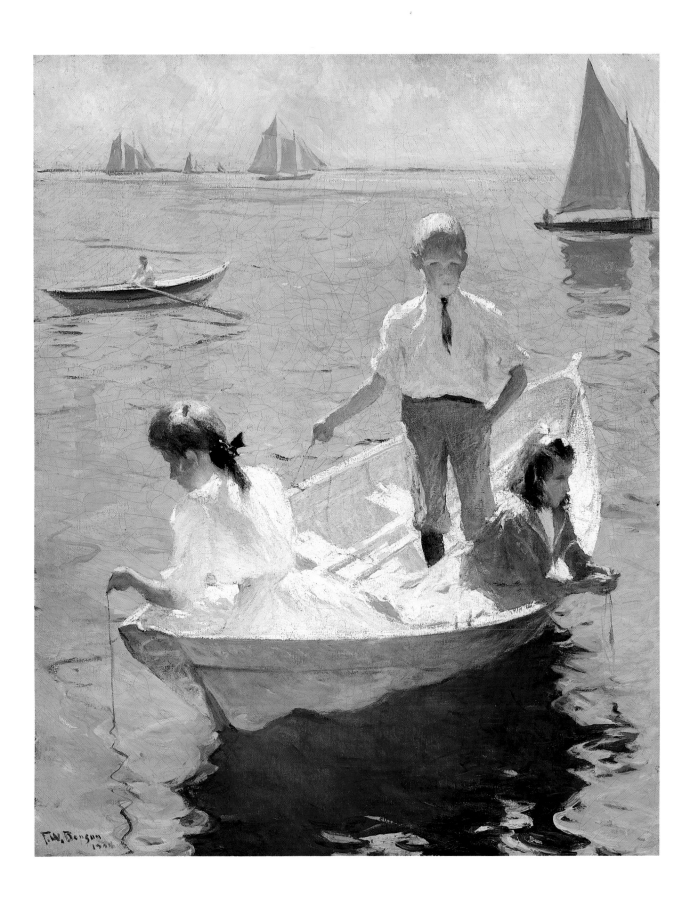

Plate 5

Children in the Woods

1905. Oil on canvas
32 × 30 inches
Signed lower left: *F. W. Benson 1905*
Collection of the Metropolitan Museum of Art,
Bequest of Miss Adelaide Milton de Groot, 1967

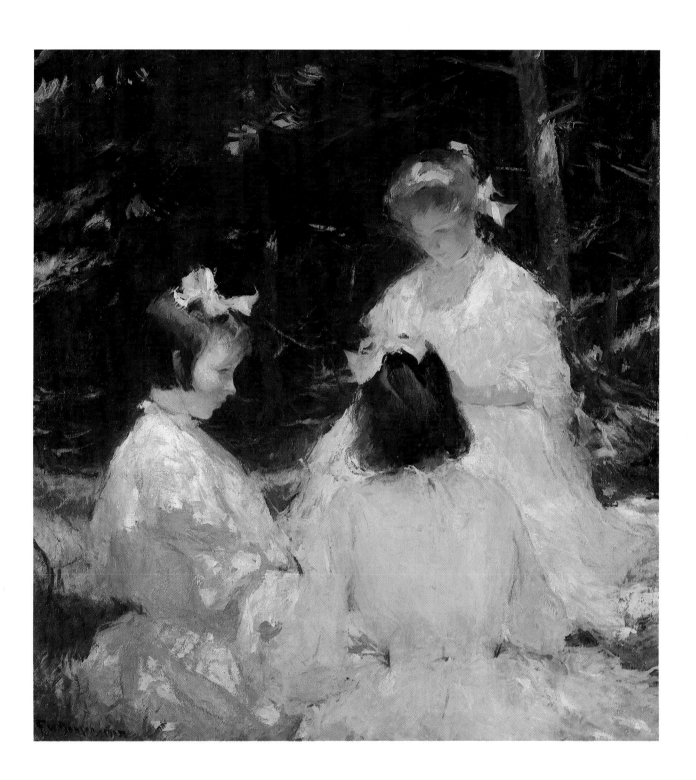

Plate 6

Laddie

1908. Oil on canvas
36¼ × 30 inches
Signed lower right: *F. W. Benson 1908*
Collection of the William A. Farnsworth
Library and Art Museum, Rockland, Maine

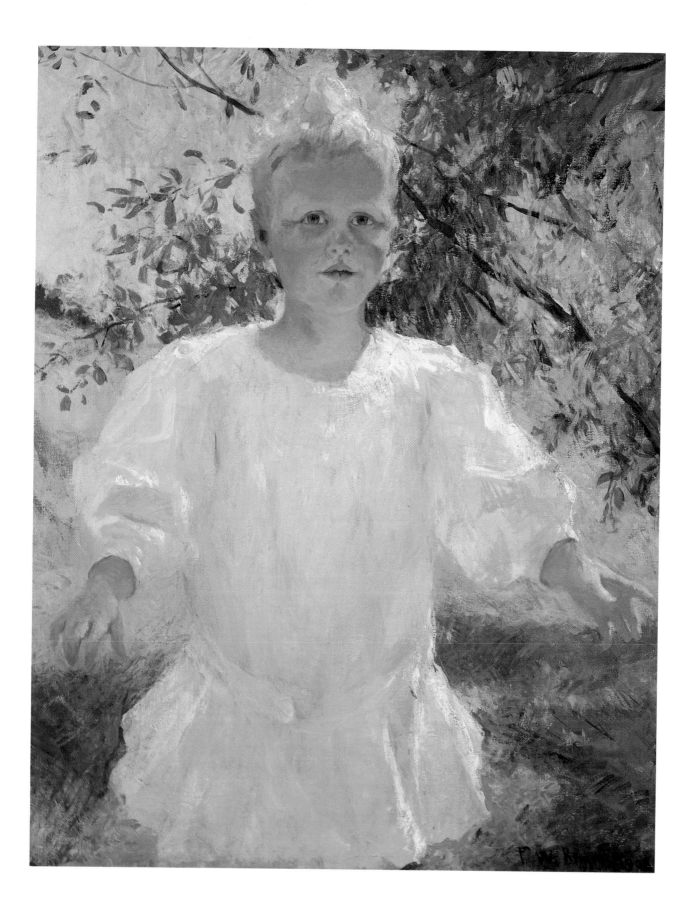

Plate 7

Elisabeth and Anna
    Alternate title: *In Summer*

c. 1909. Oil on canvas
32 × 25 inches
Signed lower left: *F. W. Benson*
Private Collection

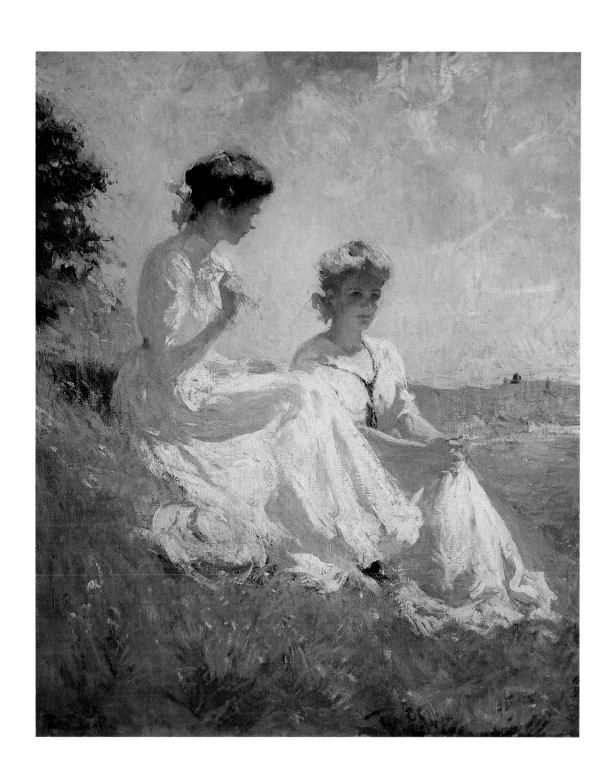

Plate 8

Woman with Geraniums

c. 1910. Oil on canvas
28 × 22 inches
Signed lower right: *F. W. Benson*
Private Collection

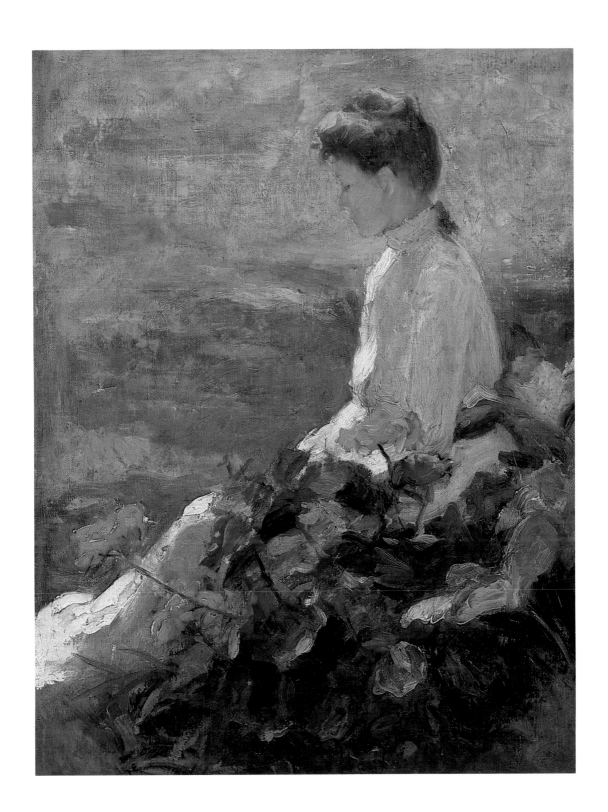

Plate 9

Summer Day

c. 1911. Oil on canvas
36⅛ × 32⅛ inches
Signed lower right: *F. W. Benson*
Collection of Mr. and Mrs. Raymond J. Horowitz

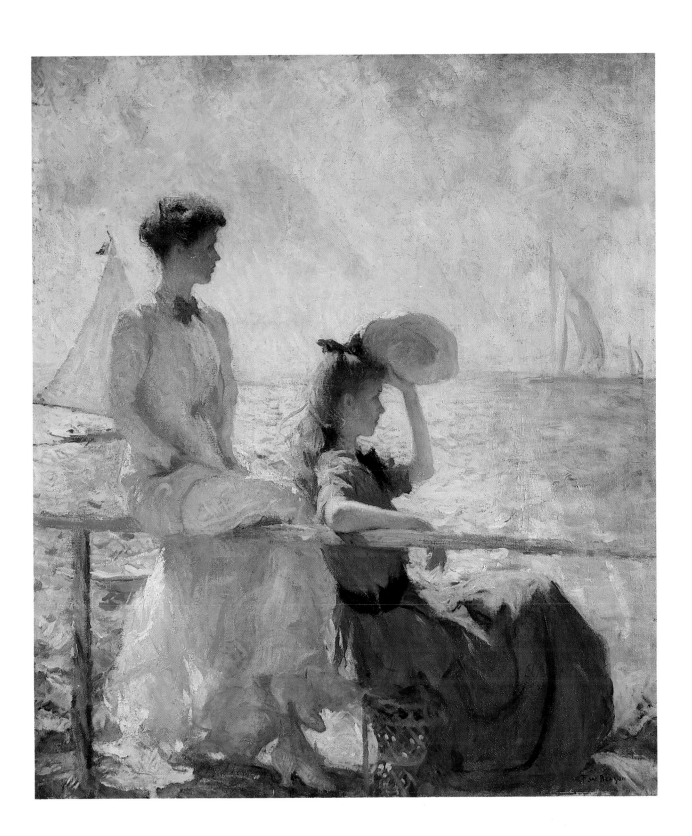

Plate 10

Afternoon in September

1913. Oil on canvas
25¼ × 30¼ inches
Signed lower right: *F. W. Benson 1913*
Collection of the Natural History Museum
of Los Angeles County

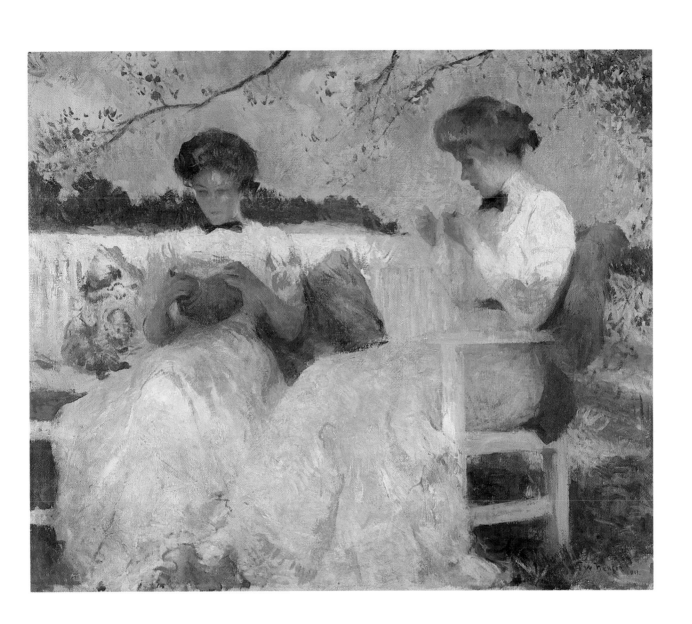

Plate 11

The Hill Top

1914. Oil on canvas
40 × 32 inches
Signed lower right: *To Elisabeth and Max,*
F. W. Benson 1914
May Family Collection

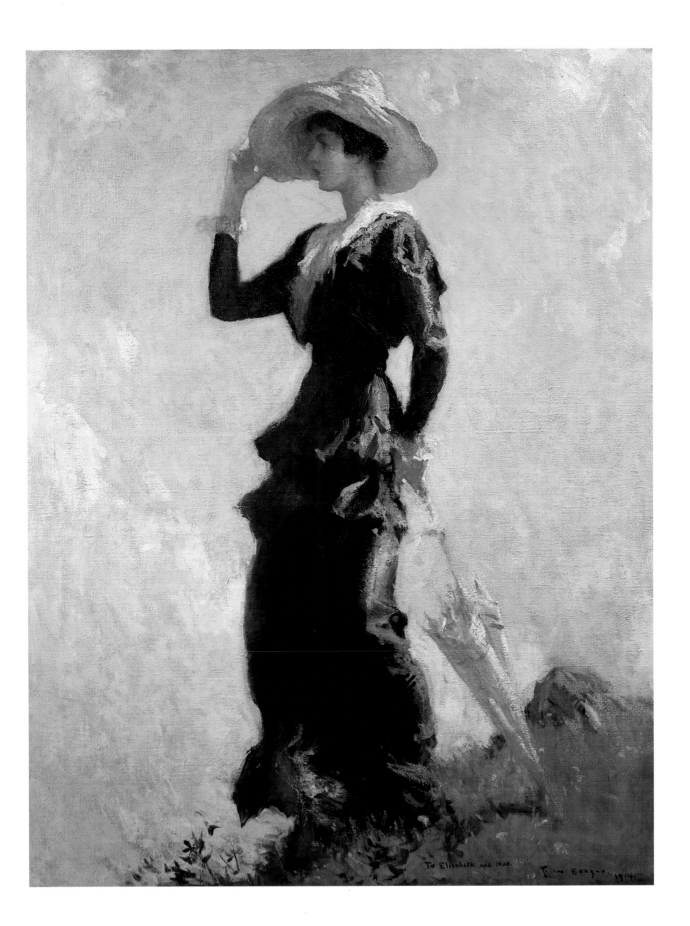

To Elizabeth and Max.   Frank Benson. 1914.

Plate 12

Eleanor and Benny
    Alternate title: *Mother and Child*

1916. Oil on canvas
36 × 44 inches
Signed lower right: *F. W. Benson 16*
and lower left: *F. W. Benson*
Private Collection

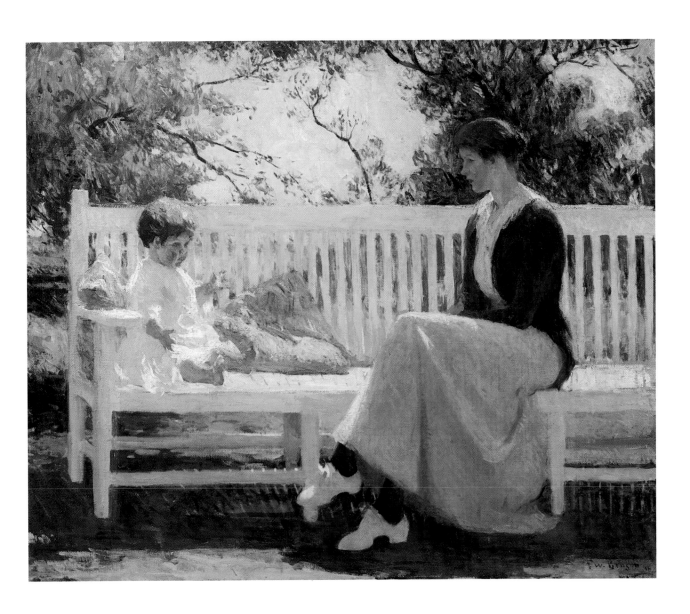

Frank W. Benson's Impressionist Paintings:
A Selected Bibliography

MANUSCRIPT SOURCES

Salem, Mass. Essex Institute. James Duncan Phillips Library. Frank W. Benson Family Manuscript Collection.

SELECTED BOOKS AND ARTICLES

Caffin, Charles H. "The Art of Frank W. Benson." *Harper's Monthly Magazine* 119 (June 1909): 105–114.

Coburn, Frederick W. "Frank W. Benson's Portrait of My Daughters." *New England Magazine* 38 (May 1908): 328–329.

Dodge, Ernest S. *Frank W. Benson*, 1862–1951. Exh. cat. Rockland, Me.: William A. Farnsworth Library and Art Museum, 1973.

Downes, William Howe. "Frank W. Benson and His Work." *Brush and Pencil* 6 (July 1900): 145–157.

————. *Paintings, Etchings and Drawings by Frank W. Benson*. Exh. cat. Washington, D.C.: Corcoran Gallery of Art, 1921.

————. "The Spontaneous Gaiety of Frank W. Benson's Work." *Arts and Decoration* 1 (March 1911): 195–197.

Exhibition of Paintings by Frank W. Benson. Exh. cat. Boston: St. Botolph Club, 1900.

Exhibition of Paintings, Drawings, and Etchings by Frank W. Benson. Exh. cat. Boston: Guild of Boston Artists, 1917.

An Exhibition of Paintings, Etchings and Watercolors by Frank W. Benson. Exh. cat. Pittsburgh: Carnegie Institute, 1924.

Fairbrother, Trevor; Stebbins, Theodore E., Jr.; and Vance, William L. *The Bostonians: Painters of an Elegant Age, 1870–1930*. Exh. cat. Boston: Museum of Fine Arts, 1986.

Ferguson, Charles Benner. "Frank W. Benson." M. A. Thesis, Trinity College, Hartford, Connecticut, 1959.

Frank W. Benson, Edmund C. Tarbell. Exh. cat. Boston: J. Eastman Chase [Gallery], 1891.

Haley, Kenneth. "Frank Benson as Colorist." *Apocrypha* 1 (1974): 14–16.

Leader, Bernice Kramer. *The Boston Lady as a Work of Art: Paintings by the Boston School at the Turn of the Century*. Ann Arbor: University Microfilms International, 1980. Ph.D. dissertation, Columbia University, 1980.

Lucas, E. V. "Frank W. Benson." *Ladies Home Journal* 44 (October 1927): 16–17; 194.

Olney, Susan Faxon. *Two American Impressionists: Frank W. Benson and Edmund C. Tarbell*. Exh. cat. Durham, N.H.: University of New Hampshire Art Galleries, 1979.

Paintings by Frank W. Benson. Exh. cat. Boston: St. Botolph Club, 1910.

Paintings by Mr. Frank W. Benson. Exh. cat. Boston: St. Botolph Club, 1904.

Price, Lucien. *Frank W. Benson, 1862–1951.* Exh. cat. Salem, Mass.: Essex Institute and Peabody Museum, 1956.

————. *Memorial Exhibition of Paintings and Water Colors by Frank W. Benson.* Exh. cat. Boston: Guild of Boston Artists, 1952.

Price, Lucien and Coburn, Frederick W. *Frank W. Benson, Edmund C. Tarbell: Exhibition of Paintings, Drawings and Prints.* Exh. cat. Boston: Museum of Fine Arts, 1938.

Scanzer, Elizabeth. "The Proper Bostonians: Tarbell, Benson and De Camp." M.A. thesis, Queens College, City University of New York, 1975.

Seaton-Schmidt, Anna. "Frank W. Benson." *American Magazine of Art* 12 (November 1921): 365–372.

Smith, Minna C. "The Work of Frank W. Benson." *International Studio* 35 (October 1908): xcix–cvi.

Troyen, Carol. *The Boston Tradition: American Paintings from the Museum of Fine Arts, Boston.* Exh. cat. Boston: Museum of Fine Arts, 1980.

Index to Reproductions

Design:
Marcus Ratliff Inc.
Typesetting:
Trufont Typographers, Inc.
Lithography:
Thorner-Sidney Press, Inc.